What in God's Name Are You Eating?

What in God's Name Are You Eating?

*How Can Christians Live and Eat
Responsibly in Today's Global Village?*

Andrew Francis

CASCADE *Books* · Eugene, Oregon

WHAT IN GOD'S NAME ARE YOU EATING?
How Can Christians Live and Eat Responsibly in Today's Global Village?

Cascade Books
An Imprint of Wipf and Stock Publishers
199 W. 8th Ave., Suite 3
Eugene, OR 97401

www.wipfandstock.com

ISBN 13: 978-1-62032-573-5

Cataloging-in-Publication data:

Francis, Andrew.

What in God's name are you eating? : how can Christians live and eat responsibly in today's global village? / Andrew Francis.

p. ; cm. —Includes bibliographical references.

ISBN 13: 978-1-62032-573-5

1. Food—Religious aspects—Christianity. 2. Human ecology—Religious aspects—Christianity. 3. Sustainable agriculture. 4. Simplicity. 5. Local foods. 6. Food in the Bible. I. Title.

BR115.N87 F715 2014

Manufactured in the U.S.A.

For Janice

Contents

Acknowledgements

I HAVE EATEN MANY meals around the world, enjoying generous hospitality, laughter, and conversation with my hosts and their guests. Thank you all. I owe even more gratitude to those with whom I often eat, and talk about globally responsible discipleship, and those with whom I have cooked and those I cook for, but Gloria and Allan Armstrong, Catherine and Peter Ball, Juanita and Raoul Concalves, Trisha Dale, (the late) Alan Davidson, Zena and Pete Ely, Helen and Martin Ford, Barbara and John Francis, Patricia Francis, Barbara and (the late) Ron Gates, Caroline Heath, Janice Heath, Lois and Wayne Hochstetler, Liz and Len Hodby, Angela and Donald Hughes, Barbara and Darrell Jantz, Maggi and Alain Jozeleau, Eleanor and Alan Kreider, Sarah Lane and Mark Cawte, Ruth and Amos Lapp, the LifeSpan Community, Margrethe and Kees Lindholm, Maria Melanetou, Leabell and Wayne Miller, Noel Moules, Sian and Stuart Murray Williams, Angharad Nash, Sally and David Nash, Jean North, Yvonne and Will Newcomb, Roger Penny, Radix Community friends, Gaye Reynolds, Helen Roe and Martin Atkinson, Virginia and Abner Schlabach, Annie and Keith Shave, Phyllis and Ed Shirk, Jon Smeaton, Kathy and Jeremy Thomson, Kathryn and Philip Walker, Cathy and Brian Wheatcroft, Vivienne Woolley and the (sadly defunct) Yellow Doors Community have all been guests, hosts, fellow-cooks, conversationalists and correspondents, but most of all friends and family on this journey. Some have already read and commented on the ideas in this book, over many years—but the faults in it will all be mine.

I am also grateful to various academics, who have lent me research notes, steered me to as-yet unpublished theses or "food reports"; your anonymity is not deserved but professionally necessary. I am grateful to the BBC, whose (public-broadcasting) Radio 4 daily *Farming Today* and weekly *The Food Programme* have consistently returned to many of these issues as has the UK's *Sunday Times* in its increasing watching brief of the British diet.

This book owes its debt to all the above and many pockets of radical Christian friends, gathering in small unstructured communities. I need to thank Christian Amondson and particularly my editor, Robin Parry, at Cascade and Wipf & Stock, as well as their copy-team and readers in seeing this narrative to its present day. I am grateful to all those who have written commendations. Thanks (again) to Trisha Dale who so carefully reads my work, tries to teach me about split infinitives, and encourages me in this "currency of ideas."

Most of all, this is for Janice, whose love, Christian faith, and vegetarian values have made this gardening omnivore happy again in our simplicity of living—which ensured the book came to birth—so this is dedicated to you and all the years we have yet to share.

PART ONE

Introduction

1

Four Snapshots and a Question

THE FERRY STEAMED ACROSS the glittering Aegean to a distant island. You could tell the seasoned backpackers as those who had unfurled their bedrolls on the hot deck of the shaded side of the ship. It decanted six of us on the quay and pulled away. Three Brits, one Oz, one Dutch, and one Dane, with a common language of some English; only two of us spoke any Greek. Unlike other islands, there were no local villagers to greet us, offering to rent rooms out in its small whitewashed town. At the far end of a long beach, we laced two "bivvys" together and strung them between the lemon trees—our home until the ferry returned three days later.

That evening, the only places to eat were *estiatoria*, producing only bread and single-pot meals in the large ovens dominating the back of the owners' houses. One welcoming owner explained he had only one big meal available that evening—no choice. I ordered beers, ouzos for aperitifs, and food for all six of us. Although we had not met until boarding that ferry, we had no option but to share and eat what was served—and get to know each other. Mezes with fresh olives and tomatoes, picked in front of our eyes, accompanied that ouzo. A steaming dish appeared. We ladled out the stew and tore hunks of warm, peasant-style bread. Beneath the wonderfully spiced tomatoes, onions, and aubergines,[1] one of our number speared an unknown piece of meat with her fork, asking, "What in God's name are we eating?"

That was a great question to ask, particularly for me as a Christian. Had I ever really thought about the broader implications of my diet? It

---

1. That is, eggplant.

brought memories flooding back. Over the course of a few years, I had heard Charles Elliott, then Director of Christian Aid, speak at a variety of conferences, clergy seminars, and student events. Over the years he had repeatedly made the point that if all the world's citizens were to have life, then we should all start living like Chinese peasants. That meant a diet with a main staple (theirs was rice) served most often with vegetables but a few times weekly with a small amount of fish or chicken, all sourced within a few miles of home.

In the intervening generation, China has moved from its post-Cultural Revolution phase to a dynamic BRIC economy,[2] changing the shape of world trade. It is becoming "Westernized" in lifestyle and diet. More food variety is demanded there and more meat per capita is now consumed there than ever before. Far fewer in the 2010s live like the Chinese peasants whom Charles Elliott was calling us to emulate.

But that changing world with its global and instant telecommunication is one that has even more starving and drought-stricken people today than thirty-plus years ago when Charles Elliott was speaking so prophetically. "What in God's name are they *not* eating?" "Enough" is the simple answer and we are part of the reason why.

I was born within eighteen months of 1954's ending of meat-rationing in Britain. My Scottish childhood was a time of thrift and austerity, with the freshest vegetables coming from Dad's allotment. By the 1960s, we were in Manchester in northern England, discovering such surprises as initially yoghurt and shortly afterwards Italian rarebit (pizza!). Then other mainland European staple products made their way into our local Spar shop for the first time. Back then olive oil was something bought from pharmacies in tiny bottles for medicinal purposes. I grew up with the Sunday roast eked out for three days, New Zealand lamb and Argentinean corned beef. But when visiting my Birmingham-based grandparents, we would go to Ladypool Road's Caribbean and Asian grocers, with their oils, spices, capsicums, yams, and sweet potatoes, as well as an invitation to dip a finger into a pot of magical ghee.

---

2. In economics, BRIC is a group acronym (invented by UK professor, Jim O'Neill) for four countries in a rapidly advancing stage of leading global economic development. These countries are Brazil, Russia, India, and China, hence BRIC.

Now we grow as many vegetables as our small plots allow. We bake our own bread, using organic[3] stone-ground flour from across the county, unless our weekend guests get tempted by the Cotswold's Stroud Saturday-market baker. We choose to buy meat for our guests from an organic, free-range butcher, with eggs from friends' chickens, and honey from nearby apiaries. We swap these as well as our home-made jams and hedgerow wines to broaden our diet.

But garlic, spices, rice, pasta, orange juice, our morning tea, evening hot chocolate, and my daily coffee and banana—even if they are fair-traded—and many other things all travel too many miles. We could not survive without tinned tomatoes to supplement our annual home-grown harvest, or goodly bottles of olive oil, or tinned sardines (necessary with my cardiac meds)—all shipped across Europe. This means that we have yet much more to question—as Christians, as people, and as citizens of God's world. "What in God's name are we eating?"

Long before that Greek island backpacking trip, I had realized that *how* we eat is important. I had learned that through family gatherings, church hospitality, and shared student houses. But had I made enough of the connections? When I was at seminary, we still had three meals a day provided in a refectory, eating far too much for predominantly sedentary students. I was not the only one to see the disconnection between chapel sermons about "Christian responsibility in God's world" before trooping off to eat gut-busting dinners with a choice of wines and beers. Yet little changed.

During a lifetime of Christian leadership and ministry, I have been privileged to travel the world, receive many types of generous hospitality, and rediscover the importance of how we share food. I love to cook for others. So I used that in ministry for congregational gatherings and smaller teaching groups—people celebrate and learn better with food. I encouraged home-groups never to meet without eating together. It is far easier to say, "Come for a meal" than "Come to a Bible study or Sunday worship" and the truth is that people came. (Much of that story is told elsewhere.[4])

There was enough ground-breaking documentary evidence in this for my successful doctoral thesis at Princeton, USA. But if this is the main

---

3. In the UK, the term "organic" now has a legal meaning when applied to any food-stuff, animal or plant. It means that it has not been produced using chemical additives, whether as growth hormones, health supplements, or fertilizers/herbicides.

4. Francis, *Hospitality and Community.*

dish, there is also an ongoing huge "side order," which has to question how and what folk are eating in their everyday lives as Christians. Whether we live in the formal dinner- or supper-party or chips-on-the-wall circuits, our shopping-and-eating lives as Christians tell our family, friends, and neighbors what we think belonging in God's world means. "What in God's name are you eating?"

These four snapshots lead me to big questions:

How and why do our shopping-and-eating habits demonstrate who we are as Jesus' disciples and both stewards and citizens in God's world? This book sets out to explore those very questions—biblically, theologically, and practically. The book is set out in four sections.

- These opening four snapshots capture various points of realization that thinking people—people of faith, but particularly those who claim to be Christian—have a challenge to face up to. This will lead us to "cooking up a storm" as each of us realizes that we are part of the solution as well being part of the problem. This is the first part of the how question.

- This demands that we re-examine "the nature of the challenge." The true situation and problem issues need to be identified at a global level from our local perspective. We then have to apply our worldview, be that philosophically or from a faith perspective, to determine whether and how the case needs to be addressed. This is the second part of the how question.

- I have identified seven key issues that must have their rationale explored, to advance our own thinking. Each issue has its own chapter.

- This revolution will not be televised[5]—it will begin with you and me wanting to change the world, in God's name. This section begins with a "Start here" chapter—more than fifty ways to change and consolidate our personal diets and lifestyle for the sake of all God's people. Change will happen only as we and like-minded others develop "a global strategy," rooted in biblical thinking and the Jesus narrative. It is only as we also increasingly apply these to our everyday living that the relevance of the why question (above) will become more apparent

5. Scott-Heron, "Revolution," 77.

to those around us. Finally I offer seven brief conclusions and a select bibliography.

These words of Wendell Berry explain why we must do this:

> Eating with the fullest pleasure—pleasure, that is, that does not depend on ignorance—is perhaps the profoundest enactment of our connection with the world. In this pleasure we experience and celebrate our dependence and our gratitude, for we are living from mystery, from creatures we did not make and powers we cannot comprehend.[6]

Everybody has to eat, except maybe those stereotypical South Asian sadhus who seem to live on goats' milk, honey, and fruit juice. If we have an ounce of compassion, we cannot look at the victims of starvation, particularly children with bulging eyes and swollen bellies, without realizing what an immense privilege we have in the affluent West to choose what we eat. Even the most cash-strapped among us still have that choice. Sometimes it takes such shocking pictures of the starving to remind us of that. But what is important is that we consider both how and what we are eating as citizens of a planet with only finite resources, including food.

6. Berry, "Pleasures," 110.

2

Cooking Up a Storm

SOME YEARS AGO, A group of doctoral students regularly breakfasted together in Princeton Seminary's refectory. As several of us Brits wrapped the remains of our overlarge blueberry muffins in paper napkins to eat later with our mid-morning coffee, our American colleagues used to smile in amusement. Looking at our empty plates, one Texan said, "What I like about you Brits is that you clear your plates every time." Privately, I had been appalled by our new-found American friends' heaped plates and how much was scraped into the trash, but I was a guest in another country, seeking to learn.

British manners meant that to leave food on your plate was a sign either of disapproval or of overconsumption—in everyday language: greed. As a child, I learned to clear my plate even if I ate too much! Family friends used to say, "Eat up—or we'll have to send it to the starving in Africa" or wherever. Before I went to high school, I had learned not to overload my plate, nor to leave food, but to take only what I needed to eat.

However, as an adult, I quickly learned, in Hong Kong and then China, to leave a small amount of rice in some sauce in my bowl in order to stop the waiter from bringing another dish of tasty goodies. The classic, humorous TV advert for HSBC bank in which oriental waiters bring increasingly large eels to the tables of Western diners is unfortunately true.[1]

---

1. A quick search on YouTube for "HSBC 'Eels' Ad" will reveal the TV advert in question.

The Price of Life

My father was a poorly paid Anabaptist pastor with huge "job" satisfaction. He and my mother used to wear their coats indoors on wintry days to economize on heating costs. They both went without meals to ensure my sister and I had hot nourishing food every day. As children, we were happy, wonderfully loved but blissfully ignorant of what sacrifices were made for our good. My parents masked the cost of bringing good life to us as children.

As an adult and a pastor myself, I learned about world development and world hunger. I had a close friend who, as a nurse, volunteered to be part of frontline famine relief teams; she had to choose daily from hundreds of starving children who should be given food and help, and which ones were past saving; then she had to leave these to die in the dust. The aid agency shot some footage of this work but it was too traumatic to show to any congregation. Our pastors' conference session had to adjourn after we watched it, while folks composed themselves enough to pray before discussing what they had seen. Most of the time, the truth of what is happening does need to be made plain—even if only to the teachers and educators to "pay it forward."

Now, as a pensioner, my eyes well up with tears as I just hear that song by the Cars, which accompanied that horrific piece of 1985's *Live Aid* footage: the dying child looks into the camera, then folds himself into the ground, chewing on the dirt finally to die. That moment should have been life-changing or transformative for every Western viewer . . . tragically it was not. Every one of us has to be made aware of realities, even if some continue to ignore the truth.

In Pasternak's *Dr. Zhivago*,[2] Yuri returns home early through the sub-zero weather to find his family standing around in their overcoats deliberating when to light the woodstove to ensure he has a warm welcome. Their sacrifice is echoed today by the poor in Scandinavia, Russia, and northern America. Keeping warm, hydrated, and fed are three basic human needs alongside shelter. The price of maintaining life in climatic extremes is tough. But every citizen of the world now has to face the situation that our planet is approaching a climatic extreme from which there is no return.

A writer acquaintance of mine does his writing in a woodland cabin, heating and cooking on its woodstove, using a drop toilet yards from that hut. He collects water from the stream and firewood in the woodland as he

2. Pasternak, *Dr. Zhivago*.

9

walks the half-mile from his parked car. He uses photo-voltaic technology to power a single light, his CD-radio, his laptop, and his mobile phone. His planetary footprint there is small. However, his wife stays behind in their comfortable flat next to the hospital where she works as an emergency room doctor undertaking "compressed shifts" so she gets bursts of days off, when together they enjoy their city life or fly to the sun for city breaks or the beach. Knowing these extra facts of their cosmopolitan lifestyle gives a very different price to their life than that assumed by his many readers. But how many of us have a "green front," where we look highly credible, when any consideration of our whole lifestyle would give a very different picture?

Here are five different reasons why you must read this book—and then why you should get other copies for your friends and family.

- Most of us as adults have allowed ourselves a childlike innocence to mask the real cost of the environment in which we are cocooned.

- The tough realities facing those who do not have our power, wealth, or home-nation to have any real quality of life are often hidden from us.

- When we are exposed to this kind of truth, do we allow ourselves to change and be committed to such change?

- Are we prepared to accept the pointers the best provisional levels of knowledge are exposing, or are we people who believe we can buy our way out of trouble?

- When you—and as importantly, others—realistically assess your life-style, is it adding to the possibilities for every global inhabitant or is it taking something away from some, if not many of them?

Let's face it. We have all fallen short of what it means to be a responsible global citizen. The very fact that you are holding this book in your hands shows that you are part of a Western privileged elite with enough leisure time and health to read rather than be scratching for subsistence, every hour of every day.

The price of life is high. To those of us who have life, there is a moral imperative to enable others to share it rather than suppress them.

"My Kingdom for a . . ."

As this book approaches its final editing phase, Europe has been rocked by an internationally reported major food scandal. What was initially ex-cused as a one-off minor example has now snowballed into a Europe-wide concern, and for some a crisis of confidence, because increasingly horse-meat has been used as a masked protein substitute instead of beef.

Initially, food-testers discovered that alleged beefburgers, packaged and sold in their budget range by Britain's largest supermarket, Tesco, had revealed DNA traces of horse-meat. To their credit, Tesco then withdrew from their retail shelves all processed meat products produced by the same supplier. The problem has dramatically escalated since this January 2013 incident and therefore there will be a number of points in the book when this growing situation needs returning to.

The initial problem was traced to Silvercrest foods, which, as widely reported in the UK, is an Irish company. They in turn pointed out they sourced their "meat" as a compressed protein product from France, occasionally Spain, and often eastern Europe. Many UK consumers had never before realized the convoluted route by which ingredients for their processed food had come to them.

Both the problem and its media-reporting became more intense. Food manufacturers sought to distance themselves from becoming implicated by having their products independently tested. One major UK manufacturer, Findus, was horrified to learn not only that many of their prepackaged meals contained horse DNA but also that several contained more than 60 percent actual horse-meat. Findus issued a nationwide apology and asked all supermarkets to withdraw their products from retail sale. Findus soon named the source of their meat, allegedly beef but containing horse, as Comigel—a France-based company. Logically, questions arose about food labeling: should the manufacturer's geographical source of major ingredients in a processed meal have to be declared on the packaging?

Bravely, an originally Dutch but now pan-European supermarket chain, Aldi, recognized that they sourced nearly all their UK processed meat from Comigel's French or Luxembourgian plants, via the Spanghera pan-European meat processors, and therefore tested all their own-branded products. Aldi had been selling prepackaged "beef" lasagna, which was discovered upon testing to be 100 percent horse-meat. Aldi then withdrew all their own-brand meat products from their stores. Comigel then admitted it had bought meat from a Romanian abattoir. Immediately France and Sweden forbade the ongoing sale of any product with meat from Comigel. Within a few days, companies in Germany, Denmark, Norway, and the Low Countries were considering similar bans.

11

Broadcast food programs and consumer groups were left asking huge questions. There are health implications: if horses are not raised for the meat market, they can be administered drugs causing human anemia or even carry carcinogens—we return to this on page 70. Others asked the question whether it was not time to abandon our British prissiness and openly accept eating horse-meat products just as much as we eat beef, lamb, pork, poultry, venison, and so on.

Another big point was often forgotten. Most people—not just committed cooks, gastronomes, and food writers—can easily tell the difference between meats, even when blindfolded. How many consumers had taken their "beef" lasagna back to Aldi or the Findus horse-meat products back to the store, complaining that the "beef" did not taste quite right? By this point, UK Government ministers were demanding meetings with officials from the UK's Food Standards Agency.

Nestlé, the world's biggest food producer, based in Switzerland, continually maintained it was "in the clear" in this horse-meat scandal. Switzerland prides itself on being the most organic, the European country with the highest percentage of local shopping (i.e., shopping at small shops rather than supermarkets or online). Then the Co-operative, Switzerland's second biggest supermarket, found illicit horse-meat traces in a number of its products. Nestlé was then discredited as horse-meat was found in its own Buitoni "beef" products, canned in Germany, on retail sale in Spain and Italy. Twelve major European countries are now evidentially implicated in an illegal, unregulated "food chain."

The storyline keeps unraveling. Britain's reputedly high-quality supermarket chain, Waitrose, had to withdraw its lower-price beef range because of adulterated meat. UK government ministers had to order that all processed meat products on retail sale be tested to ensure that the meat was both safe and what it was said to be on the packaging. Then it transpired that a UK-licensed horse abattoir had allegedly colluded with a Welsh processing plant to introduce lower-cost horse-meat to supplement more expensive beef in value-range meat products for both the UK and European retail markets.

The story twisted onward and will do so for many more years of court cases.

For the purposes of this book, three points need to be made.

- The more our food purchases are processed, and/or the food chain extends, the more opportunity there is for so-called "ingredient corruption."

- Consumers are gullible to believe both the packaging and labeling of our everyday food; it is not always what it says on the tin, or at least the cardboard packet.

- A product can have its taste easily masked, whether inadvertently or not, by the use of additives, spices, sauces, and auto-suggestion. How many of us, as parents, have shown our children the packet to explain that they are eating something they say they like? Labeling can no longer be trusted.

So the European horse-meat scandal will make several appearances in this book because it highlights "ingredient corruption," huge "food miles" transportation, inadequate scientific surveillance, poor "food safety" regulation and labeling, as well as our human inabilities to recognize products once processed.

What is important is to acknowledge the integrity of the supermarket chains in withdrawing not only suspect products but potentially similarly affected others, once the problem was publicly revealed. If you'll excuse the pun, this has left a bad taste in the mouths of investigative journalists. Many critics are now asking whether there are those in the supermarkets and/or food manufacturers who were aware of the problem or at least its potential, then turned a blind eye to it in the name of their employers' profits; therefore, just how long has this duplicitous practice been going on?

What became clear is that Germany spends fifteen times more than the UK on food-testing for human consumption. Only greater surveillance and increased food-testing can guard against "ingredient corruption." But in both Germany and Britain, the popular media's "surveys" showed more consumers were questioning processed meat and opting towards buying real meat at source.

This is not just some European "storm in a teacup," meaning a major fuss over a trivial matter. This is about an accelerating global problem in which the food supply can be corrupted (deliberately or not), mis-sold, and then presented as something it is not—any of this may mean that health risks are carried. Into the midst of this storm, accredited reports showed that some supposedly halal meals, supplied to the UK's federal prison service, contained pork that had then been eaten by Muslim prisoners.

Whoever we cook for, whether it is for our children or our parents or any captive audience, we do have a responsibility and a right to know what we are serving on their plates. They also have the justifiable question, "What in God's name are *we* eating?"

"Waste Not—Want Not"

When I was a child, "Clear your plate or we'll have to send your leftovers to the starving" was closely followed by, "Waste not—want not."

Over many years, from my various vegetable plots, we have eaten everything we have grown. As we are about to harvest celeriac, swedes, and turnips, we use their leafy tops to make soup. If a lettuce bolts, we liquidize it with cream and a light vegetable stock to make a cold summer soup. We finely chop carrot tops, and roast our own pumpkin seeds for garnishing salads. In every vegetable garden that I become custodian for, I build compost bins (often using redundant wooden pallets), so that there is no waste and goodness can easily be returned to the soil. Whatever the vegetable, if we cannot turn its peelings into soup or mash for the chickens or greens for the rabbits, they just go straight into the compost. "Waste not—want not."

Whether in Wales or France, I have helped smallholding friends humanely kill a pig or two they raised. We caught the draining blood in a bucket to make black pudding or *boudin noir*. We butchered the carcass, utilizing every joint possible. We boiled up the head, leftover skin, and trotters to make brawn—a kind of savory meat pudding. The dogs ate whatever was left while the bones from a Sunday pork-joint were made into stock. Each time, it really is a case of "waste not—want not."

An English Mennonite friend's Chinese wife discovered that her workplace managers were changing their great-quality carpets for a new corporate color. Over the next couple of days, she travelled home on the London Tube carrying a roll of carpet for somewhere in their shared house. Some Dutch friends work for the Emmaus project, refurbishing unwanted furniture for gifts to the homeless or resale to the more privileged among us. The more we can simply reuse the planet's resources, we are not causing agricultural land to be requisitioned for alternative profit nor consumer goods' production. "Waste not—want not."

For many years, I have been privileged to serve as a school governor. These unpaid, voluntary but elected posts are like school boards in other parts of the world. I did not make the best use of my school years, nor of my initial law degree studies. But I then caught the learning bug with theology—I just could not read enough history, art, philosophy, and ethics alongside my seminary studies. Lifelong learning became a passion but I realized that *should* begin in school. So I wanted to give something back. Now several times each week of semester, I am in school, supporting staff and encouraging students as well as attending business meetings. All my life's skills are utilized in different ways; my experiences are not wasted. If "paying it forward" is willingly exemplified, it teaches that we all have something to give for the enrichment, even empowerment, of others. This all helps change the world. "Waste not—want not."

For this book, these four points are clear:

- Every day many people and communities waste food products that can always have use—even if (and we can never say "just") enriching the soil.

- If we choose to eat meat (see chapter 7), we have to be responsible and ensure that nothing is wasted.

- When we start to adopt a "whole earth" lifestyle, we waste less because we see opportunities to recycle more everyday items.

- In that lifestyle's philosophy, we have to recognize our own abilities to "pay it forward" and use our personal skills and abilities, which have benefited from others' resources.

Why?

The questions with which this book seeks to wrestle demand that we ask questions about the resources at our disposal. We are global consumers—just open your kitchen cupboards or look in the fruit-bowl to check that out.

There is a storm of protest, asking, "Why has this happened?" among thinking people in all developed nations when their national aid agencies highlight the latest disaster, drought, or famine and people needlessly starve when the world has the resources to make the changes to give them life.

Those who work from any kind of major faith perspective have an implicit global vision within that faith. Whether it is in the central Islamic demand to give alms to the poor, whether it is in the Hebrews' Ten Commandments, or whether it is the teaching of Jesus (of the Christians), whose challenge is to "love your neighbor," there is an explicit expectation to take responsibility in our relationships with and for the rest of the world's citizens.

We return to the question of global inequalities at several points in this book. Anyone who declares a faith with a vision of and for the global community can no longer be simply a spectator in the "food debate." We have to get out of the bleachers (the stands) and get to work on the pitch with others. This is not a game, but something far bigger than the Superbowl, the Cup Final, and the Ashes Test rolled together.

We have to be prepared to ask the question of ourselves, question our food-store managers, undertake the necessary research in our region, and change the priorities of both ourselves and others that the "world might have life," as stated by Jesus, the prophet recognized by Islam, Judaism, and Christianity. My Anabaptist-Mennonite Christian perspectives apply all Jesus' words to our earthly patterns of following him, not simply limiting this to some future, beyond-this-world perspective.

The only way to change priorities is to "cook up a storm." This means ensuring that each of us, our households, and our close friendship or kinship groups join in the struggle for change so that the world can eat. This book seeks to help you create that discussion.

PART TWO

The Nature of Our Challenge

3

Global Concerns

IN JANUARY 2013, THE shocking news became public that 50 percent of all the food produced worldwide or nearly two billion tons of food, is thrown away annually across the world.

British readers have little room for complacency. In 2005, UK supermarkets sent 500,000 tons of edible food to landfill. In that same year, the food industry consigned seventeen million tons of edible food as "waste." This included misshapen fruit and vegetables, badly packaged goods, and so-called "meat waste." Other larger nations' (e.g., USA's) readers need to recognize that their country is not just as proportionately bad, but probably worse. Only New Zealanders, Australians, and black South Africans throw away less food waste per capita than in the UK.

Apologists tried to massage the figures away. In the "developed world," this waste was blamed on the (general) public desire for healthy food, encouraging the use of early "sell by" dates or supermarkets to demand uniform size, shape, and taste of products or bulk buying ("buy one—get one free") promoting unnecessary surplus purchasing. In the "less developed world," blame was attributed to poor storage or lack-of-transport-to-markets or simply local surpluses of "the wrong crops."

However, whatever reasons the "spin doctors" postulated—the shocking truth was there. Half the world's food was and is being wasted.

Yet within a day or so of all this becoming public, a UK-based aid agency coincidentally wrote to me asking for my help, financially and politically, to alleviate world hunger. It is popularly believed and told that a starving person dies every four seconds[1]—yes, fifteen for every minute of every day—because of the effects of hunger and malnutrition. To save you math, that is 900 people every hour, or 21,600 every day, or over 6.5m every year.

As a Western "developed world" reader, try imagining a settlement near you of 900 or a small town of 21,600 and imagine the scandal if one of those was wiped out every hour or every day (respectively) in your country. Some aid agencies believe the problem is bigger than this.

A Backdrop of Concern

When a right-wing British Prime Minister, David Cameron, addresses the United Nations Assembly about world hunger, global headlines result. When that same Prime Minister declares the fact that one billion of the world's citizens living on a dollar a day is a disgrace to all thinking people,[2] the message is clear. Action is needed. A global response to such a level of poverty is needed.

Since 1960, global food production has increased by over 135 percent yet still, in 2014, 800 million people (or 11.5 percent) of the world's current population are officially malnourished or starving because of lack of food. In 1960, the United Nations and the United States Census Bureau estimated that the world population then was between 3.15 and 3.4 billion; the uncertainty is because politically closed countries (e.g., China) did not release figures and less-developed nations (e.g., India) did not have accurate census statistics. For similar reasons, it was less possible for international aid agencies to estimate the 1960 percentage of officially malnourished people, although UK agencies (such as Oxfam) believe the global malnourished percentage has grown significantly, given the increasing divide between "the haves" and "have nots" between 1960 and now. Cities cover 2 to 4 percent of the world's surface, according to different commentators or assessments, yet all agree that the world's cities' inhabitants "consume" over 75 percent of the world's resources. In 2009, for the first time, global city/urban inhabitant figures (3.41 billion) surpassed the number of those living in rural communities. Recognized US and European population experts know that the number of cities, therefore urban inhabitant percentages, have grown since 2009. It takes proportionately more per capita resources to supply

1. Meadows, *Rich Thinking*, 127.
2. September 25, 2012.

"development infrastructure" (e.g., roads, power lines, sanitation) in rural communities than "within urbanization," therefore greater urban percentage per capita usage of resources demonstrates the developing inequality.

Every adult who reads this book can recognize the huge shift in technological change within their own lifetime. As a child in 1950s Scotland, my folks had one of the few phones in our street; now virtually everyone has a phone in their pocket. We can instantly communicate.

"In 1960, my family had a radio, no car and bought our first refrigerator; in 1970, my parents had a car, a TV and stereo record player while I as a teenager had my own record player and records in my bedroom."[3] Now I resist friends' requests that I carry a mobile phone with camera, apps, and internet access, and reject having a car that only an electronics diagnostician can service. Too many of us are buying too much consumer-technology with too much on-cost[4] planetarily.

I was a high-school student when the Apollo space program occurred, taking pictures of earth in ways my grandparents could only wonder at. Yet I was one of those participating in the challenge of 1985's Live Aid when rock stars flew between continents, performing in Britain and America. The world seemed to be getting smaller. Yet how vast was the gulf between my Western, well-fed self and that dying, swollen-bellied, Ethiopian child beamed "live by satellite" to my home TV, which inspired Live Aid. Instant communication.

Thirty years from Live Aid and a lifetime from my childhood, there can be no excuse for Western ignorance. We face a challenge. Since 2000, we have seen a number of Westernized countries—for example Japan then others—live through serious economic downturns. When the going gets tough, the majority have to accept its challenge, downsize or downshift or otherwise simplify their everyday lives.

Multinational corporations shift their production to the cheapest labor markets as never before. In the 1990s the economists' talk was all about the Pacific Rim and now, in the 2010s, it is the BRIC economies that are emerging as the market leaders. We live in a changing and global economic interdependence.

---

3. Francis, *Wind of the Spirit*, 66.

4 An alternative economic term for a negative "opportunity cost," which means the benefit that could have been achieved by a different or better use of that particular set of resources.

The nouveau rich may get richer, while the "old rich" watch their wealth and ways disintegrate. Post-war baby boomers are gradually realizing that their own children will never attain their levels of wealth nor the ability to use and abuse the world's resources as their generation has. Politicians may try to soften that, airbrush away the implications or simply deny it is really happening. What is certain is that the poor are getting poorer and their numbers are growing. I do not often find myself agreeing with David Cameron—that concord is as rare as a Mennonite supporting Mitt Romney.

A Global Community?

In North America, the posthumous publication of Marshall McLuhan's *The Global Village*[5] made it a standard textbook, acting as a benchmark for discussing the technological changes outlined above and many more. While writing this book, I received separate appeals from international aid charities for the donation of my old laptop computer—I bought my first laptop only this year. Those charities recondition them for Third World use. PV technology means that laptops can be used portably for both education and communication across the tropics.

My perception is that several of my business acquaintances believe that universal electronic communication is the ultimate factor for the extent to which the global community will be realized. They have the vision of an ostrich to think that still, when they open their food cupboards. The third snapshot of the Introduction, referring to Western larders containing eatables from across the world, reveals that. Our common diet relies on the coffee growers who fuel our business meetings or the rice harvesters providing the staple for our evening curries—but that list is almost endless. If those farmers are threatened economically, or their land is compromised ecologically, that affects me, those farmers, and my business colleagues every day of all our lives. We have to learn to think globally.

Just give yourself an extra five minutes next time you are shopping. My neighborhood store stocks Vegemite™ (Australia), Caribbean bananas, Argentinean corned beef, Canadian maple syrup, and original US Hershey bars among many products. None of this "just arrives"; it is ordered and its delivery is coordinated via the global internet. But I can also compare different supermarket prices, choose my groceries over the internet, pay for

5. McLuhan, *Global Village*.

them by credit card and they are delivered to my door. This latter option often means that we do not consider our food from its global perspective— just as endless commodities . . . and we also never have chance to check their labels. Horse-meat, anyone?

We live in a shrinking world—technologically, ecologically, and economically. We have to understand how to be part of the necessary change rather than letting the "old order of things" set the pace.

Some time ago, I abandoned involvement in the old Cold War politics of UK Left-and-Right to give some energy to the alternative "green movement." This new "landscape" was not populated by doctrinaire politicos nor the "hippies and hairies" of San Francisco's Haight-Ashbury children. Instead, I encountered folk with a holistic view of their life and this planet, many involved in local neighborhood projects and/or small-scale urban farming. Yes, it can be painful when my new-found green friends question my fifth coffee of the day or having a car collect me from the rail station. But they are in the vanguard of people asking the right kind of global questions, which we all must begin to do with sincerity and commitment for change.

If the world is going to change, it must begin with individuals taking the right steps. UK Greens often promote the "think global—act local" manifesto. A journey always begins with a first step and someone willing to make it. Are you?

World Hunger

If one out of seven in the world's population is living on less than US $1 a day, how many of them were starving on the hot evening when I spent two of those greenbacks in a New Jersey ice-cream parlor?

Most of us in the West live without any real understanding of what it means to go hungry. When I needed a particular cardiac procedure, I was forbidden to eat the night before the anesthetic. When the guy in the next bed woke up, shouting that he was starving, he was not pleased to be reminded that he was just unfortunately hungry and a hospital lunch would soon be provided.

Some years ago, a group of us co-sponsored a redundant mutual friend to go for a year to help build a school, its attendant dwellings, and a pharmacy near the north Kenyan border. He spent his days sweating to hand crank water from a deep well to mix mud and cow dung to create bricks, which baked hard in the sun. By the light of a kerosene lamp, he wrote that the villagers went without some food and water each day to enable himself and the other European volunteer workers to be fed and (literally) watered while they rebuilt that village. He broke down in tears frequently on his UK return, thinking about the sacrifice of those hungry and thirsty villagers to achieve a better life for their families. How many of us *would* or even *could* live that close to the edge?

Not all of us can have such practical reorientation. However the 1990 publication of *The Brandt Report*[6] sent shockwaves across the development and intelligentsia circles within European nations. No one who read it seriously could not want to alter their lifestyle afterwards. The fact that one-third of the world's nations not only held but also demanded the continuing lion's share of resources over the rest of the planet's citizens could not be ignored. How could rich Europeans and North Americans promote such ongoing overconsumption, of food and other resources, which would condemn so many of the rest to poverty and probably starvation?

Thanks to the BBC, the disclosure of the 1980s' Ethiopian famine conscientized a new generation through Live Aid, just as the Biafran famine had done twenty years earlier. What we are realizing only now is that sending US $50 to an aid agency is merely a "band aid"-style quick fix—it is not the solution. Wholesale change of lifestyle and consumption by northern hemisphere-influenced nations is just the beginning of the solution.

People are starving while you read this book, or while eat your next meal and argue the merits of my narrative with your friends. If you are able to throw away the appeal-for-money letters or avoid the satellite newsreels of starving children, you may as well just join the Flat Earth Society as well because you are shutting out the truth.

Diminishing Resources

In the 2010s, international conflicts occur because of the desire of powerful nations to control oil reserves. How many future generations will it be before the world is fighting over food reserves or the control of fresh drinking water?

Those of us (un)fortunate enough to go to Churchill, Canada, and see increasing numbers of hungry polar bears, while witnessing regional droughts or the increasing length of the summer season, know that climate change is happening. I recall sitting in a Princeton, New Jersey, cinema

6. Brandt, *North-South.*

where some of the vocal blue-collar members of the audience tried to shout down Al Gore's 2006 *An Inconvenient Truth*. Whether all his arguments were exact is for the academics to decide, but his trajectory is still bullet-proof. Humankind is damaging the planet entrusted to us now in permanent ways. But a decade or so on from those vocal Princeton cinemagoers, my copy of *An Inconvenient Truth* is among my frequently lent DVDs.

There is only a finite amount of oil or arable land or fish in the sea. It is no good crying when each runs out. We have to use resources wisely and prophetically *now* so that everyone gets a fair share.

Susan George's figures are often quoted.[7] Can anyone justify the 1980s fact that the USA, with 6 percent of the global population, consumed 35 percent of the world's resources? Regrettably those fractions have not really improved in the intervening thirty years. Although this book is about food, we have to recognize the interconnectedness with oil, minerals, land use, and other reserves. We will return to this interconnectedness and to transport demands in later chapters.

Before the revolution in 1949, China had 500 million people—many starved during annual famines while the real wealth was held in a few hands. During the revolutionary years the population doubled to more than one billion but encouraged the governmental development of state farms (on the Soviet model), village communes, and gave permission for private vegetable gardens. The population was fed in the manner Charles Elliott has described and advocated for the world.[8] Until the last few years of Westernization, China remained self-sufficient in food production from that revolutionary period. Starvation was used only by Mao and his cronies to control or coerce sectors of the population.[9] Yet still China has only half the amount of arable land per capita that India has. Appropriate lifestyles, correct husbandry, and just distribution of food resources do mean that the effects of fewer agricultural resources per capita can be countered.

Agro-economist Vaclav Smil's figures, which demonstrate that each human can grow all his own food on a relatively small acreage, have much to teach us (see below). If India has so much fertile land per head, political questioning means that its hunger problem is about inappropriate

7. George, *How the Other Half Dies*.
8. Elliott, *Comfortable Compassion*.
9. Chang and Halliday, *Mao*, 573ff.

organization. No wonder Gandhi based his life on collective farmsteads as a demonstrable example of both food production and simplicity of lifestyle.[10]

As we turn towards considering population demands, we also need to look at some of those countries' stewardship of resources against their rising numbers. There is little hunger or serious starvation in the crowded nations of South Korea or Taiwan, which have only half as much tillable land per person as Bangladesh and Indonesia: both the latter having rising populations. There is an agri-education needed as much across the world while the rich Westerners need educating even more to downshift their lifestyles.

Rising Population

The world has too many people in it. If we adopt Charles Elliott's thinking, we might all get fed—but not like we used to be. Globally, we have to work towards a decline in population growth, not a continuing rise towards meltdown.

It was Thomas Malthus (1766–1834) who posited that there will be a time when the rising population's basic survival needs exceed the amount of food and other resources necessary for life.[11] This concept, articulated at the start of the nineteenth century, when the global population is estimated to have been about one billion, can still act as a warning concept.

For modern-day prophets, it was Paul Ehrlich's 1968 *The Population Bomb*[12] that affirmed a Malthusian vision, predicting global famine by now, the 2010s. Thankfully, in that respect, Ehrlich was mistaken—at least, in his timescale thus far. But his book sparked population-versus-food fears among both academia and popular media. It was enough for even my puritanical high-school geography teacher to remind us that "The real problem is over-copulation!"

There is a tension. Where female emancipation and equality have occurred, birth rates are falling because women have some choice. In many Western European nations and Japan, the birth rate is falling because women are choosing careers rather than babies. In emancipated countries like Iceland, where childcare is inexpensive and easily available, the birth rate remains higher because childbearing women can easily return to jobs

10. Mehta, *Mahatma Gandhi*, 155.

11. Malthus, *Essay on the Principle of Population*.

12. Ehrlich, *Population Bomb*.

or education. Conversely, in those nations that suppress women, or restrict the availability of contraception, the birth rate is automatically much higher because babies help give women status, despite the attendant health risks and food shortages.

If there can be any good thing from the global HIV Aids epidemic, it has been its challenge to the Roman Catholic Church's support of the 1968 papal encyclical, *Humanae Vitae*. This encyclical banned the use of artificial methods of contraception by Catholics. The wide spread of HIV Aids has meant that even Catholic priests are sanctioning the use of condoms. This needs to be encouraged, not only to prevent HIV Aids but also to help limit population growth while education continues alongside to demonstrate that good agricultural practice and fewer children *mean* that it easier to feed those fewer mouths. But we must also find the money to fund HIV Aids education.

Before the cries of "hypocrite" reach me, I acknowledge that my Amish "third cousins" do not practice birth control and their movement is growing precisely because they have more children (than the rest of us). But the majority of Amish live simplified lifestyles on highly productive farmsteads, producing the large majority of their own food. Those of us who are trusted by Amish elders will need to engage them with this population concern—and soon. Folks like me who have never biologically fathered a child but have brought up several as a step-parent need to encourage the understanding that one's values can be inculcated and handed on, whatever the biology and numbers involved.

Very few thinking people like the draconian methods (e.g., enforced sterilization, or second-child removal) allegedly employed by China to stem its population growth. "One child for a couple" can sound like a mantra for some of the world's ills. But it fails to cope with natural gender imbalances (which can be caused by diet) and the rising demand for labor in an exploding BRIC economy. Population control needs to be achieved by winning the intellectual arguments for responsibility in bringing another mouth into the world. In China, the "one child policy" has done just that. China's population recognizes that this has enabled a raising of living standards for a large majority, so the birth rate has begun falling and, from 2035, China will begin facing major population decline.

There is a general principle, both historically and societally, that the more children who survive into adulthood, the fewer children parents will have. This means there is a "tipping point" when populations begin to drop.

Some Western European nations, such as Denmark, Italy, and France, are becoming worried by their falling population trajectories. They recognize healthy population percentages of children and young people, with falling infant mortality, but they look aghast at the implications of the rising percentage of those who are approaching their eightieth birthdays. High-quality health care means folk live longer, draw their pensions for longer, and therefore die at a much greater age than the preceding generation. The economic implication is that it is the "squeezed middle" who are paying for the education, health care, and social security for all. One serious option is to encourage both economic growth and (worryingly) a rising population to service longer-term national educational, health, and pension budget needs.

In January 2013, the US magazine *Slate* carried a well-researched article, quoting the results of many recognized demographic studies, including that our present global seven-billion population will peak in the mid-twenty-first century at nine or ten billion, then start falling steadily to about three to four billion by the 2300s. That will be a sustainable population, but the journey there will be uncomfortable or even deadly because war, plague, or starvation involving many *could* occur; the potential for meltdown remains as previously indicated. But if the world's present seven billion population needs cropland the size of South America to feed it, we shall need extra cropland equaling the size of Brazil to feed a global nine billion population.[13]

What is needed is a concerted global understanding so that better regional and sustainable populations occur. It is no good saying to Asian peasants that they are not to breed more labor for their rice harvest unless we (Westerners) are prepared to pay a lot more for our rice. Then, and probably only then—when a workforce is equitably paid rather than family members being cajoled, slave-like, into paddy-fields—the Eastern peasant-farmers may begin to realize that more children are not needed.

Sustainability

President Obama's inaugural address in 2013 was important for many reasons. But one of the most vital statements was his call to America to realize the need to address "climate change" questions. Visionary men like Obama know that globally sustainable change is required: "Then there are

13. Despommier, *Vertical Farm*, 82.

the environmental consequences of our fossil-fuel-based economy. Just about every scientist outside the White House believes climate change is real, is serious . . . if all that doesn't constitute a serious threat, I don't know what does."[14]

If the often-called "leader of the Western world," with access to the world's best and its greatest breadth of research, affirms the need for change towards sustainability, people need to listen. As this book has often to re-mind readers, it will take the USA to change its ways and its dependency upon so many of the world's resources if the whole world is to have life. Sustainability is often dismissed as merely the thought pattern or lifestyle of the green movement, of "doomsday preppers," of "mountain hippies," and so on, but the world is at its danger line, so sustainability has to become a mainstream and government program affecting us all. Recognizing the reality and implications of climate change is but one step towards sustain-ability—but making just one step begins a journey.

Those of us in more compact countries like Britain, Denmark, New Zealand, or the Netherlands have many more chances to encounter local attempts at sustainable living. Everyone can learn much by fostering friend-ships, creating a dialogue of ideas, with those, often extended, households who are living more sustainably than we are in our own area; they know what works and what is inexpensively possible.

As this book unfolds, it seeks to look at some of the issues that most impact sustainability. The food miles question in chapter 6 is paramount in that if the ingredients of your evening meal predominantly arrived by plane, change your diet. Meat impacts how many people can be fed, so we must ask, how much land should we use for cereal and crop production and how much for raising animals (chapter 7)? How many times will you eat meat today or even this week? When you go shopping, do you simply choose the cheapest or do you seek out those products that mean the pro-ducers are not slaves of our Western-style economies (chapter 9)?

The key issue in reading this book is to realize that *everything* you buy, prepare, and cook for your family and others and then put in your mouths raises sustainability questions.

14. Obama, *Audacity of Hope*, 168.

Eco-Concerns

It is not this book's purpose to teach small-scale farming nor ecology; however . . .

It was an Englishman named Townshend (1674–1738) who realized that yields, soil fertility, and productivity improved if crops were moved from one plot to another annually. He discovered an optimal fourfold rotation, becoming known as Turnip Townshend for his pains. Most Western gardeners still utilize a four-plot rotation—I look at such a system in my front yard through the study window as I write.

Protection from both soil erosion and soil degradation is a major eco-concern. The dustbowl backdrop to Steinbeck's *The Grapes of Wrath* is illustrative of the human and planetary costs when we get our stewardship of the earth wrong.[15]

Native Americans also knew this eco-concern as a natural part of their life's fabric. The practice of inter-cropping—growing two or more compatible types of plant in the same soil, particularly beans, (sweet) corn, and squashes—was common to the Navaho and Hopi peoples especially. They would tend a small inter-cropped plot, irrigating it well. They moved to other plots for successive years before returning to the first site.

Although questions about mono-cropping have been raised for years, the 2010s are seeing a UK rise in both broadcast and print media investigations into the practice of increasing single-crop production. Dutch friends confirm similar media trends in the Netherlands. My French home was surrounded by large fields, where in successive years sunflowers, then corn, then fallow, followed by a grassland year formed a four-year cycle. Crop rotation, in some coherent form, is necessary for the planet's health as well as our own.

Ecologically, we all know we cannot keep raping our planet.

- Popular journalism often reminds us that North Americans conservatively need three planets like earth to maintain their present consumption. Western Europeans cannot be smug as our consumption level requires two planet earths. Australasians are somewhat better but still require one-and-a-half planet earths. And these are the conservative figures.

- In 2004 Vaclav Smil, the European agro-economist mentioned earlier, published his findings that if *everyone* adopted a coherent "whole

15. Steinbeck, *Grapes of Wrath*.

earth" diet, working cooperatively, each citizen would need only 0.07 of a hectare to provide their annual food.[16] He explained that this would involve intensive labor, inter-cropping within an ecologically sound crop rotation, and using techniques that others would describe as permaculture.[17] Smil's reputable thesis rightly attracted attention—supportively from charities, NGOs, downshifters, and eco-ethicists—but there was opposition from multinationals and government economists, fearful of his decentralist conclusions. Smil's critics rightly point out that this method would involve reversing urbanization and concepts of land ownership stewardship.

- The rise of the "green" and permaculture movements show how thinking people are prepared to consider significant lifestyle change to create better and widespread quality. Loans for eco-oriented projects and house-building are far more available in Western Europe and Australasia than was the case a generation ago. In the UK, increasing numbers of town councils are gaining more Green councilors, who often can hold the balance of power in sensible planning and land-use applications.

- US-Canadian concerns over the effect of "acid rain," or Eurasian concerns over the Chernobyl meltdown, or the Pacific Rim's 2013 panic about Fukushima's leakage of nuclear-tainted waters demonstrates that countries are ecologically interdependent. We need to take seriously the Rio summit and its successors as well as their challenge to the BRIC economies that unrestricted industrial development has devastating planetary costs, threatening all forms of global life. Simply reducing our want of consumer goods helps reduce demand, therefore production and transport. If one thousand households in a settlement bought one fewer household appliance annually, they would reduce by 10–15 percent their own acid rain contribution.

- Some years ago, I stopped my New York yellow cab as we passed a community garden, where black, Hispanic, and white Americans, young and old, were together working a patch of land that had been created by building demolition. They were growing squash, zucchini, and tomatoes. They had used abandoned lumber to build a frame for

16. The *Geographical* magazine, London, January 2004 edn.
17. Mollison, *Permaculture.*

growing vegetables up the walls of the neighboring brownstone apartments. This is a vision of one small way forward.

The point is that while there are huge global concerns, as well as economic issues, each person and their own household can do something about it. That can begin with something that we all do and can review—by questioning how and what we eat.

". . . that the World Might Have Life"

I am a Christian from a radical tradition. We value the words of Jesus beyond all other teaching and philosophy. Jesus said, "I came that the world might have life—a life in all its fullness" (John 10:10). If I and other Christians are serious about following Jesus' way and living out his words, our task is to continue his intention. We can do no other than change our lives "that the world might have life," and not our leftovers.

4

Discipleship's Demand

CHRISTIAN DISCIPLESHIP IS FOLLOWING the way of Jesus. But this does not take place just at an individual human belief level, nor even that of a local community of like-minded people, but at a visionary level of actively participating in Jesus' vision for the world.

That vision is always rooted in a contemporaneous society. That vision is rooted in Jesus' Jewish background and the world of the Hebrew Bible. For Jesus' present-day followers, that vision is also mediated through the writings of the New Testament from the early Christian era. Since then, that vision has been enhanced, sometimes compromised or diluted, and sometimes corrupted by the teaching and the practice of the intervening church.

So what has all this to say about the way we eat, together and alone, as Christian believers?

Wherever we are, and whatever our faith, the nature of our diet is determined by what can be grown or bought in the locus of our daily lives. The Christian in northern Australia or Indonesia, with their plentiful fresh fruits and fertile gardens, can live more of a self-sufficient life than those in Britain or Canada and the northern-border US states.

As Christian believers, what we do and how we use locally grown food has been and should be shaped by our faith and personal discipleship. The Inuit and Indian Christian will have very different ingredients but what they do with their food must be shaped by their Christian vision. Those of us who live in societies and locations between those "extremes," with perhaps more food opportunities, have even greater responsibility in our dietary choices.

This is not simply a matter of faith but ethical philosophy, too. However, if "Jesus is Lord" for Christians, then all other things become subservient to that; even the best philanthropic ethics have to be matched or even bettered by our practice as Christians.

I have seen private video footage of Desmond Tutu, when archbishop, exhorting all his listeners in "black townships," not just Christians, to share their bread so that they could survive and struggle together against apartheid. They did—successfully.

Aung San Suu Kyi, a Buddhist and the leader of Burma's National League for Democracy, is often print-reported, or heard in broadcast interviews, referring to her childhood when her mother demanded she cleared her plate of all food she had taken, because others in their country needed food—nothing should be wasted.

 When two such world leaders in their respective struggles for freedom and democracy understand and advocate the importance of food ethics, the practice of Christians in the "free world" needs to be just as vigilant or better.

However, Christianity began in the Middle East, when an itinerant Jewish teacher and healer named Jesus called people to celebrate daily a new way of living. The fact that Jesus rose from the dead and talked of his Father in heaven set him apart from other radical prophets. Over two thousand years of history since has seen his followers declare him to be the Son of God and the second person of the triune God; those followers were pejoratively called Christians at Antioch in the first century AD. What must never be lost is that Jesus' life and societal background was in the Hebrew tradition.

The Hebrew Tradition

The first five books of the Hebrew Bible or Old Testament are known as the Pentateuch or the "Books of the Law." Within them, the outlines of Jewish dietary law are defined, but these have been refined and clarified by over two thousand years of rabbinic teaching and tradition.

Basically, Jewish Law prevents its adherents from eating "unclean animals," such as pigs and shellfish. It also demands that things are properly prepared in a particular ritualized manner commonly known as kosher. Within that kosher practice, there are demands that animals are slaughtered without pre-stunning, by slitting their throats and allowing them to "bleed out," after a particular prayer has been said over each such animal. This is known as *shechita*. Islam follows a similar practice, known as *halal*.

But Jewish Law also forbids the cooking of meat and milk products in the same kitchen or with the same utensils. In twenty-first-century homes, this means either two separate kitchens or a kitchen with each half having separate sinks, utensils, and cooking facilities. This creates a great sense of family community as adult children have to go on living with their parents, while acquiring sufficient wealth to afford such lavishly equipped homes of their own.

This no-milk-and-meat-together rule obviously has implications for wider socializing. In large US and British cities, there are restaurants run by Jewish families, observing kosher demands. Recently, my partner and I stayed in a vegetarian guesthouse in North Wales where the only other two guests were a husband-and-wife team of rabbis from southern England. We shared much animated and happy conversation about "Jewish diets," as they helpfully explained that vegetarian households will not have nonkosher forbidden foods and their kitchens would never be used for the preparation of meat-based meals.

But central to Jewish tradition and community is the practice of "eating together." This is exemplified in the Friday night meal, *Shabbat*, when Jewish families gather with acquaintances and relive the Passover narrative in a multivoiced celebration meal. When I was a high school student, I had the privilege of several invitations, which I accepted, to that eve start-of-Sabbath meal. The very fact that a Gentile Christian was welcomed and fed taught me much.

Although it is an ongoing thread throughout the Hebrew Bible, it is perhaps the book of Ruth whose narrative is most important in underpinning the Hebrew concept of care and provision for "the widow, the orphan, and the stranger" (Deut 10:18). In this story of loss, loyalty, and love, Naomi knew that her kinsman, Boaz, would not harvest to the very edge of the fields so that the passing widows, orphans, and strangers, such as Ruth, could glean and thus have corn. God's promise to Israel in the wilderness was that they would be taken to "a land flowing with milk and honey"—two signs of plenty (Exod 3:8, NIV). In their worship, Israel would have known the psalm of David which sings, "You have prepared a rich table for me" (Ps 23:5, author's translation). The provision that God makes for all his people is celebrated by the lifestyle of sharing commanded of the Hebrew people.

That hospitality goes back about three thousand years to desert tribes as they came together to form the people we call Israel and Judah. That confederation of people, throughout their suppression and struggles, has continued to celebrate their identity which their daily diet- and food-based rituals help to emphasize.

Middle Eastern Origins

Just like Christianity, both Judaism and Islam originate from the Middle East. It is hardly surprising that both these great world faiths have strong traditions of hospitality to both friend and stranger.

In today's world of mechanized transport, the desert tradition is still to give hospitality to others, even strangers. That was even more necessary in biblical times of desert travel on foot or by camel. The tradition of hospitality lives in this generation across all the shores, nations, and islands of the eastern Mediterranean—the area commonly known as the Levant.

It is no accident that the word "companion" is drawn from Roman Latin, meaning the "one with whom you share bread." It was these same Romans who occupied the land of Jesus' earthly birth. Bread-sharing was the culture of both the wealthy and the peasantry, of both the occupying forces and the suppressed. The occupying force in the Palestine of Jesus' day spoke Latin, which had that "companion" word for the "sharer of bread," which underpins the common nature of the practice itself.

Many modern Christian hymns and songs sing of hospitality, journey, common pilgrimage, the sharing of bread, and being "companions on the road." The very nature of Christian discipleship is rooted in the Hebrew and Middle Eastern traditions, which regard that companion nature of bread-sharing as central in the pursuance of faith.

The Jesus Tradition

It was into such a world that the Jesus of the Christians was born. Ray Bakke, the urban missiologist, often makes the point that Jesus, having been born into the humblest of Middle Eastern beginnings, spent his early childhood as a refugee in North Africa.[1] Perhaps, now that Africa is the continent with the greatest proportion of refugees, that aspect of Jesus' incarnation needs to take on a more important emphasis for his followers.

In terms of this book, it points to the fact that Jesus in his life was part of that world that relied on the welcome, hospitality, and provision

1. Bakke, *Urban Christian.*

of others for survival. Clearly, as homeless refugees, Jesus' earthly family was not left to starve in the north African dust of Egypt. What are we saying about the twenty-first-century global Christian community if we are content to let the homeless—who will include the widow, the orphan, and the stranger—starve in the North African dust or anywhere else? By logical and biblical thinking, that same principle applies to whomever, in whatever nation. Discipleship makes its demands upon us as part of the global community.

"When I Was Hungry . . ."

Jesus himself makes this same point to his own followers (Matt 25:35), arguing that in feeding whoever is hungry, we need to respond to them as we would to Jesus himself. In our attitude to the world's hunger and our daily diet of many free choices, do we shop, grow, and eat that "the world might have life" (John 10:10)? The evidence is further stacked against us with the death of each and every starving person on this planet.

"Give Us This Day Our Daily Bread . . ."

Some years ago, I visited an aid project in a very unfashionable and poor country in Eastern Europe, where two local churches were setting up an orphanage in an abandoned building. We had driven with a truckload of goods, toys, furniture, and medicines across Europe. We needed to take turns sleeping in the cab as others among us drove to avoid stopping for long periods when we would become sitting targets for hijackers, desperate for the material goods and drugs we were carrying. We had taken camp beds too and we slept in an unheated, sub-zero attic when we arrived. The pastor of the local church killed one of the village's last pigs to celebrate our arrival. As I preached among his congregation, the next Sunday, there was huge poignancy and meaning as we responded together in saying the Lord's Prayer, "Give us this day our daily bread . . ." Sharing the daily bread of those who could ill afford to feed us, told of the huge onward responsibility each of us Brits had on our return. Your reading of these words and the consequent challenge to your thinking and lifestyle is part of that responsibility. I have written, you have read—what difference will it make?

The Feeding of the Multitude

Very few incidents are captured in all the four portraits of Jesus' life, which the church calls the Gospels. The very word "gospel" means good news. The fact that every version of that written good news contains a scenario in which Jesus takes a small visible amount of food, prays over it, and then feeds four or five thousand people, is important. Whether Christians believe a miracle took place or believe this prompted everyone else to share their hidden lunch boxes is immaterial to my argument here.

What this "feeding narrative" demonstrates is that Jesus challenged the skepticism and suppositions of (at least) the disciples that "we have not enough food" and ensured there was enough to go around. Likewise, in today's world, we have to follow Jesus' injunction, utilizing whatever little we have for the benefit of the many. In meeting the needs of the hungry, whether short- or long-term, we have to acknowledge the example of this "feeding narrative," that everyone accepted a common diet of "loaves and fishes."

In today's world, Charles Elliott's advocacy is entirely consistent with that—except now it is the world accepting the 1960s diet of Chinese peasantry rather than "loaves and fishes."

The "Sharer of Bread"

Jesus was a great "sharer of bread." He so often visited the home of his friend, Lazarus, at Bethany, that Lazarus' sister Martha complained that their sister Mary sat listening to Jesus, while she (Martha) did all the work (Luke 10:40). In that context, "the work" would have been preparing the main evening meal for them as well as for Jesus and his traveling followers.

Perhaps one of the first Bible stories children learn is about Zacchaeus, the collaborating tax collector (Luke 19). Zacchaeus begins his rehabilitation by redistributing his ill-gotten wealth and Jesus eating with him—a sign of human reaffirmation that rejects any previous ostracism.

Jesus was often criticized as "one who eats with tax-gatherers and sinners" (Matt 9:10). Eating with others was a declaration of Jesus' kingdom—one in which all are welcomed. As a child I remember standing in a queue in the post office with my grandfather, when a neighbor criticized him for inviting some of the first black immigrants to their city back for Sunday lunch. I recall my grandfather booming out his response, "It is what Jesus would do, and so we do it too . . . brother!"

Elsewhere, I have written: "Food, and its sharing, seems central to Jesus' own ways and his revealing of the kingdom of God, in word, deed, and prayer. If being a disciple is to follow the way of Jesus, there is a significant pattern of sharing food, across the boundaries of society."[2]

Faith from a Table

It has become a theme of much helpful, recent feminist theology that Christian discipleship is shaped by a table. We can all acknowledge the Western notion underlying that—not everyone eats at tables. But the nature of Christian faith is often defined by how Jesus shared a Passover meal (a Jewish necessity) with his close followers on the night that he was betrayed prior to his torture and execution.

The task of this book is not to examine the style of that meal or its relative emphases for all Christian movements since then. However, this book aligns itself with the feminist thought that declares the community of that table, receiving the gift of another's hospitality in provision of a meal and a borrowed room, to be decisively indicative of life within the Jesus community then and now. In world terms, if you are reading this book, you are one of those whose mind, hands, and pockets can ensure there are tables provided for everyone in this world. Christine Pohl, an ethics professor, wrote: "Recovering a rich and life giving practice requires attention to good stories, wise mentors, and hard questions."[3] Are you willing to be part of the answer?

"Jesus models that 'communities of faith' must be open to sharing all that they have, however little, to reveal God's abundance. Whether a group is a community (or not) can perhaps be more easily determined by its use of resources in times of hardship and little, than it can in days of peace and plenty."[4] What a personal challenge when we know one seventh of the world's population daily faces hardship and little! Last year, I led a food-sharing seminar for some American college students. Nearly all wore wristbands, asking, "What would Jesus do?"—the equally important question is what they would now do as Jesus' followers. A year on, I wonder if they still give any thought to the implications of the nature of Jesus' diet for them.

2. Francis, *Hospitality and Community*, 12.

3. Pohl, *Making Room*, 14.

4. Francis, *Hospitality and Community*, 11.

A Christian Movement

After Jesus' death and resurrection, a movement of his followers gradually cohered. By the time of the third century, groups of solitary desert monks met weekly for Sunday worship and to eat together. That pattern was replicated throughout the European Celtic tradition and later in medieval monasticism.[5] Thanksgiving in the USA is rooted in the shared harvest meal of the "Pilgrim Fathers" and their families, celebrating God's provision for them as the first white settlers in a new land. Nowadays, sharing distinctive ethnic meals with US African American, Hispanic, Amish, or Mennonite Christians speaks of a pattern of sharing food as a natural expression of their corporate discipleship.[6] What we can begin to recognize is that there is a "Jesus-shaping" to the sharing of food, which ensures there is food for all and not just a few.

All this finds its roots in Jesus and the earliest Christian communities. The Acts of the Apostles records that the first Christian communities used to "meet together daily, for the apostles' teaching, to eat together, sharing all that they had" (2:42, author's translation). The point here is that right from the first post-earthly-Jesus days, Christian disciples were committed to sharing all that they had. Secular Roman literature commonly records this distinctive aspect of Jesus' lifestyle. Today I often end "food-sharing seminars" with this question: "If you were arrested for your Christian lifestyle, would there be enough evidence to convict you?"

The New Testament's Letter to the Hebrews, sent to some of the scattered groups of Jewish believers, states: "Do not forget to welcome and feed strangers, for by doing this you may have entertained angels without knowing it" (Heb 13:2, author's translation). Often in the UK's Mennonite Trust, we are asked to provide a meal for a group visiting close to one of our network of households. I enjoy cooking for such folks, providing good wholesome food and home-made bread in ways that demonstrate our care for the planet and its peoples.

Every time I buy fair-traded tea, coffee, rice, bananas, and so on, I am by extension welcoming those food producers, who are strangers to me, to share my life and wealth. As with every other financial supporter of international aid agencies, my money spent this way may "entertain" some starving peasant family to a life-saving pot of mealie-porridge; they are my

5. Dunn, *Emergence of Monasticism*.
6. Francis, *How Then Shall We Eat?* 25.

brothers and sisters just as much as we all share the task of being God's messengers—angels!

In that fantastic sixty-sixth book of the Bible, Revelation, there is a clarion call: "Here I am—I stand at your door knocking. If anyone hears me and opens the door, I will come in and we can eat together" (3:20). Are you hearing the voice of Jesus? Ensuring there is food to eat is central to the Jesus community. That community is impaired if not shamed by the fact that there are those who will never hear that voice except by our gift and provision. That will demand changing our lifestyles and our understanding of generosity and wealth.

Having Dominion

From the creation narratives onwards, throughout the Pentateuch, a theme threads its way concerning humankind's dominion over the rest of the created order. So often, this has been wrongly used to justify the rape of this planet, wrongful subjugation of its creatures and to create an arrogant individualism that presumes God will never allow humankind to run out of what it needs to survive.

Bob Dylan, the songwriter, included a song entitled "Man Gave Names to All the Animals" on his 1979 *Slow Train Coming* album that actually showed the lie of such wrongful interpretation. In that song, he explained how it was humankind who gave each kind of creature both its name and its importance within God's created order. Having done that, humankind is responsible for their care and respect. That in simple terms is exactly what "dominion" is.

There are three key words—respect, care, and stewardship.

- Respect: When I tend (note the verb) my garden, I have to ensure that I rotate my crops, enrich the soil, and plant my seeds in due order, thus respecting the natural order of a growing creation. When I worked as a veterinary wrangler, the way you handled a tiger or a domestic cat demanded similar skills but different distances and strength to respect the relative powers of teeth and claws.

- Care: In growing many of our vegetables, I take care when picking out fragile seedlings or take care if any of my smoking acquaintances offers to help with the tomato harvest—nicotine damages tomato plants. When looking after our folks' chickens, I take care to ensure that they have shade on sunny days and are locked away by dusk so they are not easy prey for our neighborhood's foxes.

- Stewardship: I collect as much rain as possible in water butts to irrigate our crops—saving me money on my water bills, which I can then use for something else. If we make too much jam or pickle, we swap it with our local friends and neighbors or sell it at charity markets. We have to realize when a chicken is past its egg-laying life; then we feed it up well so it can feed us well too.

If we apply those terms to our food:

- Respect: Do you respect the need for animals to live lives encountering fresh air and pasture rather than the confines of crated intensive production? Do you respect the producers of your exotic goods (e.g., rice, tea, coffee, bananas, and citrus fruits) as brothers and sisters to insist they are paid a proper and fair price for their goods?

- Care: Do you care how your meat was slaughtered? Do you care how much nonstandardized fruit and vegetables your supermarket buyers consign to landfill?

- Stewardship: Do we allow our kids and even ourselves to leave food on our plates? How much food do we overbuy then waste? Are we good stewards of the land which is entrusted to us as owners and tenants?

If you have had any moment of hesitancy over these questions, you need to think again, then read on, helping yourself to work out how to change things.

We can apply this to a much bigger planetary canvas.

- Respect: If we truly believe that God is both our and the world's Creator, what are we saying about our faith if we act as though that which God has given can be abused for our own selfishness? To be explicit, we live in God's world, where there is enough for all unless a privileged few succumb to the sin of greed. If you are reading this book, you are one of those, as the Hebrew prophet put it, "living amongst those with unclean lips" (Isa 6:5).

- Care: This is about educating ourselves, our community and our nation to exercise proper care over the world's resources. This will mean not demanding so much burning of fossil fuels (think of personal and food transport as well as the way we heat our homes), which then damages the ozone layer, creating global warming, and on it goes.

- Stewardship: This is an extension of our understanding of global care as it is reflected in our commitment to the equitable use of the world's resources. The biblical word is "stewardship," in all its facets. It means sharing what we have. For Christians, it is listening to Jesus' words: "If anyone has two coats, let him give one away."

Having dominion is just as much about how much we keep in our wardrobes or how many vehicles are in our garage as how much food we waste from our pantries and freezers as well as where and how that food is sourced.

What Does Biblical Stewardship Mean?

The preceding sections can start to give pointers to us about the nature of biblical stewardship. It needs to begin with a balanced reading of Scripture and prayerful discussion within an outward-looking group of believers, who can trust each other enough to work through their arguments, politics, and differences.

Perversely, before the big questions can be wrestled with, some small steps need to be taken.

- Can that discipleship group always discuss things after sharing an everyday meal and the necessary tasks of preparing it?

- Have we enough trust in those friends and acquaintances to hear that we might be wrong?

- Are we prepared to recognize that the high school student might have better researched the facts than the pastor in this multivoiced conversation?[7]

- Are we prepared to undertake the reading or make the lifestyle and shopping changes or even grow more of our own food?

While we may not be able to do much more than exercise our voices and votes, buy less imported food or drive fewer miles, we need to consider

---

7. Murray Williams, *Multi-Voiced Worship.*

the big picture.[8] The facts of global warming and how we share life[9] as well as changing global economic patterns[10] need to become part of our discussion's agenda at some stage—but these cannot be explored properly in this volume. Biblical stewardship cannot be divorced from the world. In seriously thinking about these issues, it may well challenge the way we think about God.[11]

Biblical stewardship means being able to recognize wrongful patterns of "dominion." For visitors to mainland Europe, it means recognizing the destruction necessary for the artificial creation of pre-Revolution formal gardens at Versailles, Vaux-le-Vicomte, and elsewhere in the style of Le-Notre and his students. Similarly, visitors to Britain can see an equivalent reshaping of natural landscapes by Capability Brown at many of its so-called stately homes. Zoological students can recognize the shift in attitudes of, for example, the five zoos and aquarium of the New York Zoological Society, from the poor dominion "stamp collection" model of solo and pairs of animals to the present-day, much better, dominion practice of keeping familial breeding groups by a seriously minded conservation body.[12] Equally, we need to repent of how much Christian wealth, either side of the Atlantic, was built upon the trade and labor of black slaves as well as repenting of the "transport" and harsh treatment of convicts exiled to Australia. Our past is full of wrong dominion.

Therefore, we need to be significantly objective in our study, our discussion and our lifestyle changes to create better patterns in our biblical stewardship today. No longer can North Americans and Brits live as though we have three and two planets' resources respectively to sustain our lifestyle. No longer can we leave half our dinner on the plate while the homeless of our cities raid the bins behind the restaurant. But the starving and significantly poor seventh of our world cannot raid our bins; they can rely only on hope that we can and will change the order of things. That means some new thinking in the biblical stewardship of our lives; seeing the world through God's eyes and reflecting upon the injustices we take for granted.[13]

8. Ward and Dubos, *One Earth.*

9. McFague, *Life Abundant.*

10. Daly and Cobb, *Common Good.*

11. McFague, *Models of God.*

12. Scheier, *New York City Zoos.*

13. Meadows, *Rich Thinking.*

A Christian Diet?

The point has already been made that we all have to eat. The question is, how? Then, what are the implications of our growing, shopping, and eating for *all* of our sisters and brothers across the world? It is no good for those of us in the northern hemisphere's snowbelt to spend all winter growing tomatoes and citrus fruit in hothouses, which add to the problems of global warming.

There can be little support to create a "Jesus diet," but Jesus' followers need to do everything in their power to create a "Jesus-shaped diet." What I mean is this: any thinking person realizes that Inuit, Australian, Minnesotan, British, and many other nationalities of Christians cannot create nor sensibly source the diet of a first-century Mediterranean peasant, such as Jesus. So, "the" or even "a" "Jesus diet" is not possible for the majority of world Christians today.

But every one of those world Christians can allow Jesus' values in his respect for the planet, his advocacy of "care for the neighbor," and his reliance on sharing food to shape the way we grow or produce, shop, then cook and share our food. Therefore, I can easily advocate that every world Christian must have a "Jesus-shaped diet."

There are those like Charles Elliott who will therefore rightly argue for a downsizing of our Western lifestyle, as previously described. I tried that diet for one Lenten season, only augmenting it with coffee, tea, and breakfast cereal—several of my proposed weekend guests postponed their visits until after Easter. But I did make many significant and lifelong changes to what I eat and what I feed my guests.

There are those like Stephen Webb who staunchly advocate that Christians move away from meat-eating and adopt vegetarian lifestyles.[14] But while he acknowledges its benefits to the global community, his initial concern began from an animal rights "wrongful dominion" perspective.

There are those biblical scholars like John Dominic Crossan who excel in explaining Jesus' own non-exploitative omnivorous diet and itinerant lifestyle, rooted as it was in the first-century Galilean culture.[15] But however much we wish to or could downshift, that lifestyle is no longer possible, even in twenty-first-century Israel and Palestine, with all its nuanced sophistications.

14. Webb, *Good Eating*.
15. Crossan, *Historical Jesus*.

What we have to do is begin again. The next section of this book takes several wide-ranging issues—one per chapter—reflecting upon some of the concerns involved. They can only raise principles and issues involved. The responses that can be made will be diverse because your location matters. If you live in a city apartment or as a Florida snowbird or as a Scottish crofter or a Queensland permaculturalist or just in burbs with some usable backyard, your answers will be different.

PART THREE

The Big Issues

5

Water, Water, Everywhere

MANY YEARS AGO, SOME friends and I were backpacking in the Spanish coastal Pyrenean region and strayed into the Basque country. The locals seemed immune to the laxative qualities of their own well water. Bottled water was hugely expensive. It was cheaper to use the local sparkling white wine to clean our teeth each day. If I did not know it before, I knew from that moment how precious a commodity is good, healthy drinking water.

On another trip, I wandered down an alley leading away from a north-west African tourist market. I emerged into a shanty town. There was an open ditch running down the middle of the muddy street—it was full of sewage and human detritus. A woman appeared from one of the roughly built dwellings and picked up a hose from the ground. Turning a tap on the wall, she filled a cooking pot, she dropped the writhing hose and its end flopped into the ditch. People do live like this.

Coming through Hong Kong, we went to a gaudily lit restaurant-boat in the midst of the harbor with its floating rubbish, rotting carcasses, and oil-slicked surface. We had a great meal on distinctively patterned plates. Returning to the dock by sampan, we passed a hatchway on the back of this restaurant. A kitchen hand was dunking baskets of these same plates in the harbor's water to clean them.

The Water Scandal

Seventy percent of the world's surface is covered by water. Most of that is seawater but, due to climatic convection, it continually "re-circulates" as rainfall. However, because of industrial, commercial, and nuclear pollution, hydrologists vary in their estimates of how much of that 70 percent is potable, recognizing it may only be between 8 to 17.5 percent of the total depending upon where in the world you are. Humankind requires good fresh water to live. We cannot afford to waste water. One future apocalyptic scenario is that wars will be fought over water then as nations fight over oil now.

Water is a natural resource and morally should not be owned by companies, private or multinational, because it belongs to the peoples of the world.

I am a regular, monthly financial supporter of the UK charity, Water Aid. I applaud its international aim to dig wells, provide locally maintainable pumps, lay quality pipes and provide fresh, drinkable water to increasing numbers in the developing world. But I also support its British aim to encourage every UK household to become financial contributors to its international aim and work. To help to educate Brits while ensuring others have what we just accept as a right is vital if we are to be global citizens. As importantly, if every household became a Water Aid financial supporter, it would help every family, every consumer to recognize something of our global responsibility.

There are parallel charities in North America, mainland Europe, and Australasia. How many of us have cause to be thankful for the safe, fresh water available from our taps as we brought up our children or live our daily life today?

Why is it that clean, drinkable water, whether a cupful or a gallon, costs five times more in Nairobi than in any North American city? Why is it that three gallons of water provide the daily drinking, washing, and cooking water of one person in the developing world yet in the USA flushes only one toilet?[1] Why is that more than one billion people do not have access to safe drinking water?[2]

It is a scandal that, internationally, the developed nations are not working hard enough, fast enough, or cooperatively enough to ensure that every child, every parent, and every citizen of the world has access to safe, clean drinking water. It is, after all, one of the core stipulated human rights declared by the United Nations, and people of all faiths have always seen giving water to the thirsty as an issue of right living.

1. Fisher-McGarry, *Be the Change*.
2. Meadows, *Rich Thinking*, 127.

It says something about the so-called developed world that we waste excess amounts of water. I am a trustee of a charity that owns several properties—we try to ensure that every WC cistern is both dual-flush and contains a water-saving device. Not everyone can yet live by the "if it's yellow let it mellow, if it's brown flush it down" maxim but the day may yet come when we have to. Any of us who has done field research—archaeologically, ethnobiologically, or primatologically—knows it takes about a month to become resocialized to using the flush when we return to so-called civilization.

During the Midwest American drought of 2012, I was struck by the lack of water butts and recycling aids in comparison to what is just a normal everyday occurrence in most Australian homes on the edge of cities, and not just in the outback.

The twin roofs of my home collect all rainfall into water butts for use on my yard's vegetable plots, beds, and containers. During the winter, in our household, when we have to use more canned goods to supplement the harvests in our freezer, we use water from those butts to wash out the cans for recycling. My household's small, only vehicle has its lights, screen, and windows cleaned weekly with that water too. If we use a car-wash, we make sure first that they recycle all the water they use. All this is easy to do, if you take time to think, act, prepare, and ask. Our water butts paid for themselves in one growing season, with the saving on using tap water from the regional water supplier. The economics work in your and the world's favor.

When I go into a restaurant, I always ask for tap water to drink with my meal. If they try to charge me for it, I just quietly ask the manager to justify the price—then pay it. I certainly do not want either to pay over the odds for it or to drink some nondescript overcarbonated product that hits my pocket and will give me "gas" for the afternoon or overnight, which then adds to global warming. Gradually, my business colleagues, friends, and family are enjoying the merits of tap water again and adopting my stance.

There is a con about bottled water. In the summer of 2012 in Britain, both Asda (owned by Walmart) and Tesco (Britain's largest supermarket chain) admitted that their budget-price—Smart Price and Every Day Value respectively—bottled, still water is simply filled from their production plant's domestic supply. Across many producers, even more expensive aerated water has just a few ingredients or pretty packaging to justify its hyperinflated pricing. "Think what you drink!"

A Cordial Welcome

When I lived in southern France, we experienced the temperatures of Australia's northern territories, southern California, or the American Midwest. One of my regular calls was to a household who made their own summer cordials. They used home-grown plants like liquorice and lovage, hedgerow fruits and meadow flowers, each making piquantly flavored cordials, which when bottled air-tight kept for months. To be offered a cordial, diluted with iced tap water, and sit on a shady veranda was a good way to conduct the business in hand.

If this was a cookery book, I would offer recipes and methods for making cordials. But now, back in southern England, I know many other households who use local natural ingredients to make the cordial base for refreshing, additive-free cool drinks. Such a beverage is a healthy alternative for all ages, keeping adults from daytime alcohol and children from so-called fruit squashes full of additives, sugar, and (still in some countries) damaging cyclamates.

Later, we shall return to some questions about fruit juices. But what must be recognized in everyone's diet is the need to have a balance of foodstuffs. For English people to eat too many of our native apples at once tends to give one stomach ache before one will be poisoned by too much fruit. But this is not true when excessive consumption of fruit juice occurs. Speak to any dentist and they will easily give warnings about young children being given a surfeit of natural fruit juices—particularly when parents think they are providing the healthy option. The problem is that many supermarket cartons of juice are made up from concentrate. This is imported into the country of sale, then sugar and warm (tap) water is added in a giant blender before chilling and packaging; just look on fruit juice cartons to actually see what you and your children are drinking.

Cordials or an individual piece of fruit, with less innate harmful sugars, are far better than most factory-reassembled fruit juices, which can cause dental caries, if not overconsumption of sugars and vitamin C.

In early 2013, the UK's Royal College, which represents all the UK's doctors, called for a significant tax on all carbonated sugary drinks, because of the sugar affinity if not sugar addiction they cause.[3] At the same point they advocated a ban on the addition of extra sugar to fruit juices. By September 2013, support for this had broadened to include dentists and social workers as well as nutritionists and politicians. The intention is that

3. *Metro*, January 29, 2013.

this begins with producer-initiated high-profile labeling of sugar-contents, although some multinationals are refusing to make this industry-wide, which may precipitate legislation and a potential tax per can.

Yes, while we can afford it, the glass of orange juice at breakfast is a good idea. But I am always reminded when staying with Amish families or in Bruderhof communities, how good cold water or a diluted cordial or home-made lemonade tastes in a work break on a warm day.

"No More Tea, Vicar!"

There is a very English joke that if a conversation veered onto risky or even risqué ground, when the vicar (or priest) came visiting, that everyone could be distracted by the request, "More tea, vicar?" That phrase is used in some families, with no clergy present, as a warning when the conversation veers towards the unmentionable.

During the twentieth century, much more became known about the production of tea and coffee. The fact that the majority of tea-pickers were virtually slaves or that coffee-growers were subjugated as peasant farmers does not sit easily in the conscience of faith. The caricature of the English as inveterate tea-drinkers, or the idea that American society runs on coffee, survives because they are not far from truth. However, the issues of faith, justice, and global partnership are returned to in chapter 13.

In Westernized culture, tea and coffee are everyday beverages that friends and family gather around. But they exemplify a Western ignorance about the nonfinancial costs of their production.

The Indian subcontinent produces over 80 percent of the tea used by Westernized nations. That same subcontinent was covered by 20 percent forest in 1960 but by 2010 that had decreased fivefold to only 4 percent, because of the increased demand for land for human habitation, subsistence farming, and commercial production of, predominantly, tea and rice. In that deforestation, local wildlife populations are being not just threatened but destroyed, disrupting the ecosystem.

The macro-example of the Indian elephant is illustrative. Elephants live in matriarchal family groups, traveling together, obviously needing large amounts of space, and vegetation to consume. The destruction of their habitat forces elephants out of forests into rice-paddies and tea plantations, where they destroy the vegetable plots of workers, who retaliate, splitting the herds into dangerous and homicidal subgroups. The Indian wildlife authorities are shooting five times more rogue elephants now than a decade ago. Recently, the BBC World Service carried an interview with an Indian economist, advocating a tripling of the price of tea to create both an economic and an ecological adjustment in reducing the Western demand for tea.

One only needs to be scared by a Colombian bus ride or a jeep ride through Jamaica's Blue Mountain tracks to see the carnage—vehicles, dead pack-animals, and human grave markers—to realize how dangerous it is to bring coffee beans to Western distributors. I have no way of assessing the truth of a South American aid worker's public lecture in London that alleged every adult who drinks five cups of coffee a day for a fifty-year adult life has probably been responsible for the death or maiming of one coffee-grower or carrier or a member of their families. I lift my eyes from this text across the desk to my coffee and have to speculate on what price it has really cost. Do you do that?

Milk

When I first went to high school, one of my classmates was the son of a Pennine hill-farming family. Very early every morning he and his father would milk twenty or more of their thirty cows, each known by name, with a portable machine, before that boy walked two miles down the lane for a fifty-minute bus ride to school. Their farm is gone now—the land was sold to house commuters to Manchester. Now the smallest UK dairy farm struggles to be viable when milking 120 cows daily, each known simply by a number, while maintaining their other "dry" (nonlactating) stock.

In England and Wales, 80 percent of the milk produced by farmers sells to one of three dairy distributors, who have gradually swallowed up their smaller competitors. In turn, these three giants process and package the milk for all the main seven supermarket chains. This creates a cartel and, if the larger chains use milk as a "loss leader" (selling below the price of production in order to attract customers), it is the farming producers who have to take the hit of nonviable prices for their raw milk.

Dairy Crest, one of those three giant milk processors, publicly admits to its shareholders that it can make money on cheese and butter production but not on simply processing milk. Everyone's profit margins are falling. Recently I spoke to a farmer in our county who admitted that his only employee, a tractor driver who does the "relief milking," takes home more money in a week than that farmer has in a fortnight.

Since 2000, UK dairy farm numbers have dropped from about 29,000 to the 2012 level of 14,800 with a further twenty closing down each week. Various factors emerge. The UK dairy industry is bracing itself for a 50 percent cattle-feed price hike because of the 2012 US Midwest drought, compounding the increasing rise in feed costs.

As part of this book's research, I visited a large dairy farm with over four hundred cows. As cows come into the automated milking parlor, barcodes on their plastic collars are read electronically, so the food hopper receives their individual level of supplement as their udders are machine-sprayed and the milking cups automatically attach to their teats. All this is controlled by one operative in a clean white coat, on a glass-walled gantry, pressing buttons and looking at each cow's yield on the screen. What a distance from my student milking days, standing in a pit, hand-washing each cow's udder, under swishing tails and the "manure shower."

The European Union is removing its agreed milk quotas[4] for each member country. The surplus of one milk-producing nation literally pours into neighboring nations where the supermarket competition for milk prices is at its most intense. Each year for the past decade, Britain has been the only country consistently in the top three of such supermarket competition.

Already the Irish Government are planning for post-deregulation with their Harvest 2020 initiative to increase their milk production by 50 percent. This relies on Ireland's wet climate to enable dairy cattle to be grass-feeders, reducing production costs while creating a surplus for export. In the Netherlands, the home of the Holstein-Frisian dairy stock, similar initiatives are being nationally considered to help their export balance of payments. Across Europe, dairy farming is now classed as agri-business even if not referred to as an industry.

Federal Europe is a helpful microcosm of the world's regional scenarios. If Westernized lifestyles are promoted as the ideal, involving greater milk consumption, North America will have interstate price wars for dairy commodities, just as Australasia will as part of the Pacific Rim nations. These regions are beginning to recognize that this will be their forthcoming scenario.

---

4. An EU agreed milk quota is the amount of cows' milk that a member country is allowed to produce with an EU subsidy via its national government.

"Pure as Mother's Milk"

I was walking with a group of pastor friends up a Scottish mountain (a Munro![5]) on a hot day. Perspiring hard and nearing the summit, we came across a small, crystal-clear, tumbling burn where we drank deeply. "Pure as mother's milk!" exclaimed one colleague. Thirsts quenched, we had not climbed another twenty feet when we found a rotting sheep wedged into the rocks channeling that same stream. The colleague who had carried bottled water from our overnight hotel laughed out loud.

Since I was a primary schoolchild, fifty years ago, a public debate has raged in Britain about whether all public water supplies should be fluoridated, and if so to what level. Fluoridation is the addition of about one part per million of fluorine to the public water supply to help combat tooth decay. It is undertaken alongside other statutory water treatment demands so that the supply can be officially listed as "drinking water." All domestic UK properties are expected to be connected to the cold-water main public supply of "drinking water." Readers of this book in other Western-styled countries will recognize similar national statutes and public debates.

Popular discussions about Western-styled infant-rearing have argued about the relative merits of breast-feeding or not. It is normally true that men who advocate "breast is best" are either lazy (no need to share the night feeds) or, wisely, have an enlightened sexuality, as they are quite content for their partner's breasts to maintain the changed shape breast-feeding brings. The alternative is to use "formula," either concentrate or powder, which needs to be made up with clean water to provide safe nourishment for newborns and infants.

For many years, I was a staunch supporter and passionate advocate of the boycott of Nestlé products. Neither the evidence nor the company's apologetic statements could mask the fact that they were supplying baby-milk or "formula" freely to maternity units in the underdeveloped world. New mothers who gratefully used these stopped lactating themselves, and therein was the trap. When they returned to their home villages, they had to buy these Western products, which often they could ill afford. Worse still, the majority had no access to the clean water that these products demanded to create safe nourishment for their babies. And, yes, some babies died while others became malnourished.

---

5. The "Munros" are those 282 Scottish peaks over 3,000 feet in height; there is a challenge among hill-walkers to achieve all these summits in their lifetime.

There was a huge Western boycott of Nestlé products over this "baby-milk scandal." But this became increasingly difficult as the multinational company's tentacles were revealed embracing (then) Swiss Lindt chocolate, French Perrier water, Crosse & Blackwell's salad products, Buitoni's canned goods, as well as many other brands including their own proprietary brands. Even though Nestlé has cleaned up its act and the coordinated international boycott has ended, I still do not knowingly drink Nescafé (coffee), nor buy their confectionary or other products—neither do many of my friends and work associates. What does "pure as mother's milk" mean?

In Scotland, statutorily all milk has to be pasteurized—that is, to undergo a heat treatment for fifteen seconds at 77 degrees centigrade and then be super-chilled—to remove harmful bacteria. Those various "bugs" can be far more than just harmful as they can sometimes cause major illness, and occasionally death, so there are strong public health arguments for mandatory pasteurization.

In England, Wales, and Northern Ireland, milk has to be pasteurized before it leaves the farm for onward sale via one of those three dairy-processing conglomerates. But in these three countries, milk can also be sold "raw," that is unpasteurized, at the farm gate. I have rural Cotswolds hills acquaintances who buy "raw" milk by the jugful as they undertake the daily school run. One reason they do so is because pasteurization also kills the enzymes that help the milk's lactose-lactase transition in the human gut. If that transition does not occur, it makes that person more susceptible to diabetes-like conditions.

In April 2014, the US federal courts began to hear cases brought by Maryland farmers against those Amish Pennsylvanian farmers who were allowed to sell raw milk and transport it across state lines, whereas the Maryland farmers are legally forced to transport it only after pasteurization.

However, townies like me have no option but to take the risks and buy pasteurized milk, or go vegan. Pure as mother's milk is only a truth for calves or fortunate country folk in most of Britain and parts of the USA. So how much do you want your milk to be processed?

"Water, Water Everywhere, Nor Any Drop to Drink"

Human and other mammalian physiology cannot exist without water ingestion. What this chapter has sought to say is that whether that water is taken in as it comes directly from the tap, or cold (flavored by cordials, in fruit juices or milk), or hot (as tea and coffee), there are both health and ethical considerations involved in each individual's consumption.

The task of every person of faith and/or morality is to ensure that every world citizen does have the most inexpensive and ecologically justifiable access to water. Otherwise, they will and we may be echoing the cry of Coleridge's "Ancient Mariner": "Water, water everywhere, nor any drop to drink." The violence and carnage caused by India's rampaging elephants will be as nothing if the world begins to fight over water as it now fights over oil—a scenario previously mentioned.

We have to learn from the Arabs and Spaniards of previous generations and build huge underground cisterns for water storage. We have to learn from the Australians and the "green movement" and recycle and retain more water for secondary usage. We have to learn from American "doomsday preppers" that low-tech but inexpensive well-drilling is a task not just for the survival of a few but that "the world may have life." All this can begin with you today as you "think what you drink."

6

Food Miles, Free-Range, and Animal Welfare

How far has your food travelled before it arrives on your plate? How has it been produced and at whose expense? These three questions should animate the minds of every thinking consumer.

Food Miles

When I lived in rural southwest France, I had huge consumer choice. The two regional markets—five and twelve miles away—each had over thirty food stalls weekly, even over the winter, more than doubling that in the summer and early autumn. The stallholders were local producers of vegetables, fruit, eggs, cheese, poultry, and other meat, from their own or neighboring small family farms. The supermarkets in both those towns made no apology for selling similar regionally produced products. French supermarket vegetables and fruit were often misshapen but always tasty, in marked contrast to the blander homogenized and standard-sized crops available in UK and US supermarkets.

As I returned to the UK, I took longer with my shopping, checking product origins while discovering that my "local" Farmers' Market sold vegetables produced well beyond our region. My French sojourn had sharpened my mind to the "food miles question." But the issue is not clear-cut.

Readers living in non-metropolitan North America or coastal Australasia can easily recognize:

- the availability of local produce markets and the ability to buy locally sourced fruit, vegetables, and daily meat;
- the dilemma of other retail suppliers, presenting a wholesome image while sourcing many of these everyday products from large distances;
- the need for many everyday foods—tea, coffee, bananas, etc.—to be sourced via importation.

We all have to wrestle with the "food miles question." Although we return to the issue of self-sufficiency in a later chapter, it is a very disciplined or hardy individual who can choose to abandon all tea, coffee, and other imported goods in favor of their localized vision.

Quantifying "Food Miles"

What is a "food mile"? You might be surprised how often that question is put to me at conferences.

A "food mile" is no less nor more than the mile you walk, cycle, or ride. What makes it distinctive is that it measures the distance that each individual food product has come from where it is produced to cross your kitchen to a plate on your table.

Sometimes, at conferences or summer camps, I invade the kitchens or food stores (by prior arrangement!) with groups and we calculate the food miles of each product being kept for that group's use. One recent UK exercise yielded 4,500 miles each for coffee and sugar, 4,000 miles each for tea, bananas, and rice, each of five different spices took 3,800 miles and the cans of tomatoes and beans took 3,000 miles per product, Italian olive oil and Mediterranean sardines were each 800 miles, and the north African oranges took another 1,000 miles. For those products only, that adds up to 48,600 miles. But the problem is that there were a whole host of seemingly also necessary products from the Americas or Asia in that British food store.

Excepting the youngest primary schoolchildren's understanding, the argument above is obviously principally flawed as none of these commodities is imported as a single item but as part of a bulk package. But if, for example, one thousand bunches of bananas were imported, this still creates four air-miles (i.e., 4,000 ÷ 1,000). If the consignment of Italian olive oil was four hundred bottles, creating two air-miles (800 ÷ 400), it is easy for anyone's store of food to easily add up to a number of miles. Obviously, the math will not be that simple or the quantities so few or uni-dimensional, but the illustration is vital. Using figures supplied by my neighborhood's green grocery and general convenience stores, most suburban family households, even with the exact quantities and math computed properly, will be at least in double-figure miles, for an average store of food. This is because we often forget the final few or part-miles for each single item, from the shop to our home. Rural households will obviously have higher "food-mile totals," because of the longer final supermarket-to-home unit mileages involved. When that is multiplied by the number of households in our street or neighborhood, the size of the problem can be realized as one that needs addressing.

Green beans are the classic and most quoted example because the UK buys nearly all its extras from one tropical country. About 60 percent of the green beans produced in Kenya, or £40 million in monetary terms to them, are destined for the year-round UK market. What is needed is more government intervention to gradually reduce the window for such imports, while subsidizing new Kenyan agricultural developments for local markets as UK consumers eat a more responsible and seasonal diet, which can and should include UK-grown green beans in the summer. Similar logic can be implied for other everyday vegetables, like broccoli from other tropical countries or year-round hothoused tomatoes from the Channel Islands. Why on earth are shrimps/prawns from the north Atlantic flown to South America for processing, then to Thailand for packing?

When the world is 24,901 miles in circumference at its equator, think of the cost of moving your store of food from its many geographical sources. How many times can you afford to go around the world, collecting up enough for your family's need? Now multiply that up by the number of separate households in your street, settlement, or suburb and the figures become astronomic.

"Something's Gotta Give"

Putting it simply, the world cannot sustain, financially or ecologically, this level of global consumption. In the well-known phrase, "Something's gotta give." I remember walking outside my Western-style hotel's compound in Indonesia, through the nearby village, where craftspeople sold their wares by kerosene lamps from their front verandas, breaking off from their family meal to do so. In marked contrast to the five-course indigestion that I was walking off, they were eating much more the "Chinese peasant" kind of diet which Charles Elliott had been advocating. "Something's gotta give."

Excepting the Gulf states, when I travel in the Islamic world it is far harder to recognize a division between rich and poor than in the so-called Christianized West. Islamic peoples dress in the same style without ostentation. Alms for beggars can just as much be food as coinage. It is caste-bound Hindu India or drought-ridden sub-Saharan Africa where I most easily recall the truly starving on the streets. Food inequality is not just a problem for the West. But it is the failure of the West to live up to its expected Christian and egalitarian ideals that so inflames extremists to want that inequality replaced by an Islamic caliphate. The "food miles" question is a global issue with distinct political nuances. "Something's gotta give."

Inevitably, fuel, shipping, and freight costs are rising. But it is not just about how a product comes to your country—there are trade issues and what the producers are paid for getting their hard-won product to the wholesaler, the port, or the railhead. So you have to count the mule miles or the Asian ox-cart just as much as the containerized shipping or the air-freight miles.

Britain is blighted by ever-larger container trucks that bring single or a few products from ports to wholesale distribution centers. But then similar-sized lorries then transport a mélange of products to local supermarkets, often returning empty. This is a huge waste of fuel as a global resource. Similar practices occur on larger continents like America or Australia and the refrain goes up: "Something's gotta give."

For some years, a colleague lived within a few miles of the southeast UK's biggest importing point. His local supermarket's products passed his door to be driven 250 miles to a distribution center, from where mixed lorries returned to that supermarket less than a mile from his home. This book cannot offer a one-size-fits-all blueprint for different countries but seeks to inspire enough local questions so that national reviews and debates occur.

Working towards Alternatives

But there is hope:

- Many small towns in Midwest America or rural Britain have had to question how long their communities can be "jammed-up" by juggernaut supply lorries being given the sat-nav shortcut.

- Groups such as churches or human rights activists, among many, are questioning the values of a nation that prides itself on tariff-protectionism and/or "free trade" rather than "fair trade."

- Many Western families are changing their patterns of consumption—often in simple ways such as growing vegetables or keeping chickens in the backyard.

- Every individual reader of this book can do the "food miles" count on their store cupboards and decide to change things.

Just reducing the use of *one* long-distance product or selecting the local alternative *per year* (spices have to count as one product!) will make a real difference over a decade. If during that decade *you* persuade one more household each year to adopt the same reduction practice, and similarly influence others to do the same, *your* initiative alone will have reduced the food miles on fifty-five products.

During my French sojourn, a Dutch neighbor bought a small fertile field just outside the village, upon which he developed a *potager* or vegetable garden. I often met him, pushing his loaded wheelbarrow home for lunch. He exchanged vegetables, eggs, and honey for other villagers' produce. He joked about "reducing food miles for barrow-metres." I looked at him quizzically. Apologizing he asked whether the English had barometers to check the incoming weather. "A lot more barrow-metres and a lot less food miles are what the world needs," he said. He is right and he will be even more so in future days.

Free Range

But it is not the whole story. I grew up near northern Britain's Pennine hills where virtually free-range "hill-beef" was reared and only fattened on coastal plain pasture for a few weeks before slaughter. This kind of farming with beef-suckler herds has been lost, but it was a viable cooperative way for the more-coastal Cheshire Plain dairy industry to deal with its surplus animals. Of course, this assumes that dual-purpose (beef and dairy) cattle can serve both milk and meat industries rather than some remaining with the overbred dairy breeds, with increasing high milk yields, in use now. Rethinking global solutions to the human diet will require the reintroduction of such regional solutions to the food industries.

An Exmoor acquaintance raises free-range suckler calves to produce beautifully marbled organic beef yet he won't supply any shop more than twenty-five miles from his farm. We need more like him. I do have my favorite butchers across Britain[1] but nothing compares with knowing the cuts you want and checking that meat comes from free-range, organically fed animals.

The Animal Welfare Factor

The Hebrew and Christian traditions both understand the biblical injunction that humankind has "dominion" over animals. Much interpretative debate ensues about humankind's treatment of its fellow creatures on this planet. What are the limits of such "dominion"?

Jews and Muslims have strict dietary laws, forbidding the eating of pork and shellfish, while advocating no pre-stunning of animals for slaughter. Buddhists and Hindus observe a "sanctity of life" principle so some animals are regarded as sacred; hence the phrase "sacred cow."

Christians tend to be guided by an omnivorous principle, defined by Peter's experience at the Roman centurion's house in Joppa (Acts 10:9–16). There Peter had a dream of a blanket, containing all manner of creatures, lowered down from heaven, while being told, "Kill and eat." It is the human demand for the butchery business that requires slaughter. That, in its turn, demands that we question how animals are kept.

Intensive Stock Production

As a teenager, I worked as a veterinary assistant. We regularly visited a farm that had intensive veal crates containing calves. These young animals had been prematurely taken from their mothers, and were kept totally indoors, fed supplements, and not able to exercise nor turn around. I have not eaten veal since, nor learned to cook it. Regularly, during that employment, we visited pig units, intensively rearing piglets for slaughter at fourteen to twenty-eight weeks old, depending upon whether bacon, ham, sausages, or pork joints was to be the ultimate product. I still cannot reconcile the word "dominion" with those two examples.

We also had to deliver preventative "treatments" to intensively reared stock. The worst experiences were among intensively kept poultry. These

1. In Highworth, Abergavenny, Bridlington, Ludlow, and Tettenhall.

long low sheds are often spotted in the UK and US countryside but within them the sight and smell were bad; often dead, dying, and deformed birds just lay where they fell to rot.

The UK TV chef Hugh Fearnley Whittingstall changed the chicken-buying preferences of Britain with three one-hour 2008 Channel 4 TV programs. In them, he exposed the waste and horrific scandal of intensely produced chickens. Within weeks, supermarkets were reporting that the demand for ethically produced, often free-range, chicken had increased tenfold. It is not enough. Even deep-litter beef steers raised indoors never felt the weather nor ate grass—two things their Creator intended. Keep asking your questions.

Telling Porkies[2]

In Denmark, I visited a huge pig unit where mating, birthing (in small crates), and rearing all took place indoors under artificial light; the only time the pigs walked outdoors was down steel-railed walkways to the onsite slaughterhouse. "It may be life, Jim, but not as we know it." This farm—with its farmhouse, concrete drives, whitewashed buildings, and flower beds—belied the mechanization and large-scale commercialization of such pig production. Similar narratives can be given to beef, lamb, and poultry hybridization and large-scale production.

During World War II, the British Government fostered pig-clubs when street-corner bins were used to collect food scraps, used by the local pig-club tended by local neighbors; a little relaxation of some legislation and this could return.

The days of the backyard pig seem gone, yet pork remains possibly the large meat-animal that most folk can help to produce. When I was at primary school, all the scraps from our school dinners were scraped into the "pig bins" and collected every couple of days by a local pig farmer to feed his stock. There can be dangers if diseased and/or inbred pigs eat pork scraps in quantity, but these can be avoided. Today, it is illegal in the UK, the Netherlands, and Denmark to feed household scraps to *any* pig, and in Britain it is illegal to move any number of pigs without paperwork submitted three weeks in advance to a government department. Madness.

---

2. "Porkies" is Cockney rhyming slang for lies (from "pork pies"); this is colloquially used to indicate truths are being evaded.

However, the UK is unlikely to return to its pre-war high of four million pigs. Putting that figure in perspective is the fact that today, Denmark has 12 million pigs but only 6 million people; obviously the huge majority of that pork is for export into northwestern Europe. Approximately 10 percent of the UK's pork is produced by one British "farmer" who almost single-handedly bred the commercial hybrid Meidan pig with its long body and sixteen (instead of twelve) teats. How you ethically view such hybridization to increase litter yields and therefore pork production demands your serious consideration about what "dominion" means. The majority of the rest of Britain's pork is imported but if it is processed and/or repacked here, it is still often labeled and sold as "British."

However, another issue for Christians and other thinking people is about the market's impact upon animal welfare. In September 2012, eleven thousand more breeding sows were sent for slaughter than in September 2011 because of the high price of animal feed. Therefore, as food economists expected, the UK price of quality pork and bacon virtually doubled in 2013, while some supermarkets obscured this via subsidy or changing product sizes and packaging. However, the price of commercial pig-feed across Europe continues to rise, ultimately being converted into higher retail prices.[3] The implication is that the remaining breeding herds will have to be "more efficient" if farmers are to maintain profit margins. Will this lead to less pork products, or less meat generally being eaten? If less animal feed is required, can that grain and other feedstuff be utilized for human consumption?

Don't Forget the Backstory

I have lived in southwest France, where production of foie gras took place in every village. To watch a neighbor force a funnel down a goose's throat and cram grain into its gullet was not the kind of "dominion" I believe is biblical. The artificially fattened goose livers are processed then canned for sale. Sometimes our meat products are so presented that we forget their backstory. Familiarity may breed contempt but not enough people are familiar with the issues involved in putting meat on their plates.

Recently, the European Union has outlawed the practice of egg production from caged chickens. This was euphemistically known as battery housing. Regrettably, many of these battery cages have since been resold

3. BBC Radio 4's *Farming Today* program—September 24, 2012.

for commercial rabbit meat production. One key answer to good animal welfare in meat production is to buy only free-range or wild-shot meat.

This kind of "animal welfare" argument is one of the three coherent reasons why some vegetarians choose to be so; we return to the others in the next chapter. Unless we can guarantee the proper welfare of animals and foster this debate among other thinking people, whether of faith or not, meat-eaters put themselves on a slippery slope in any discussion about the "dominion" or "right to keep animals" debate. That is why we also return to the "animal welfare" debate in the next chapter.

There can be no excuse for shipping live animals halfway across the globe or even across Europe. Meat should be reared locally and organically before humane dispatch within a few miles of the animals' birth-farm. Of course, meat will cost us far more to buy but both our principles and humanity need to be observed in the proper care and nurture of any creature destined for our tables.

7

The Big Meat Debate

What Made You Decide to Eat That?

ARE YOU A MEAT-EATER or a pescatarian or a vegetarian? Perhaps you are vegan; that means eating no meat, no fish, any animal products or derivatives at all. How did you make that choice? Through your faith, or some other ethical basis? Or did you not like the taste or what you have heard about food production?

The Jesus View

If Jesus ate the Jewish Passover, he ate roast lamb; therefore he was a meat-eater. After his resurrection, he asked for a piece of broiled fish to eat to prove he was alive, therefore he was a fish-eater. There are enough biblical references to Jesus eating, sharing bread, and picking crops to know that food was a vital part of his everyday life and of that of his followers. We have already reviewed the "Jesus diet" in chapter 4. If we claim to be Christians or Jesus-followers, these simple examples show that we cannot use Jesus to determine whether we should be vegetarians or meat- and fish-eaters.

Cheval

Assuming you are not vegetarian, what meat would you eat?

In France, horse-meat is an everyday staple meat—available in supermarkets and specialist butchers (*chevalines*)—and is known as *cheval*.

Historically, the British do not slaughter and eat horses but do send live horses across Europe for precisely that purpose; and five UK abattoirs are licensed to slaughter horses and can sell their meat onwards. Some Native Americans regard the horse as the embodiment of an animist spirit, and therefore sacred, so *cheval* is not a regular US meat source, but it could be (although it is illegal to slaughter any horse for human consumption within the USA). Australia has enough brumbies to consider the same question. In comparison to some African or Asian cultures, Westernized nations *tend* to be more emotive about what can be and what should considered to be a meat animal.

As previously noted on page 10, there has recently been a global food story that an Irish meat-processing plant had been found with traces of horse DNA, in some cases 29 percent of the total DNA, in the beefburgers it supplied to Britain's largest (Tesco) and other budget supermarkets. Good investigative journalism recognized that this may have been brought in within "protein powder additives," used to bulk out cheap burgers, imported from Europe.

What also became evident is that many US horses are bought by "kill buyers" who export them to Canada and Mexico for slaughter before the meat is 90 percent-plus exported to Belgium, France, or Italy, where it is openly sold as horse-meat or processed into horse-meat or "protein powder" additives. Another allied concern is that in the USA, horses are regularly treated with an anti-inflammatory drug, phenylbutazone (known as "bute"), which even in minute quantities is a human carcinogen.

Cheap burgers: as Jesus said, "Which father among you would give your child a stone when they ask for bread or a snake when they ask for fish?" My concern for the poor is not that they will perhaps eat horse inadvertently but that they might give their children known carcinogens. "What in God's name are you making your children eat?"

However, all this highlights hypocrisy in British and North American contexts. In Britain, Dartmoor is one of our best-loved national parks and famed for its feral ponies; at least three hundred of these are culled annually and are sold as meat for both human or animal consumption, but this has only just been publicly revealed.[1] A similar North American hypocrisy is in the work of those kill buyers highlighted above.

---

1. BBC Radio 4 *Farming Today*, September 22, 2013.

Disney™ and Other Stories

Disney™ has not always helped parents encourage children to eat available meat. How many urban children will not eat Donald Duck,* Bambi* (venison), or Thumper* (rabbit)? But if you grow up in Chesapeake Bay, England's west country, or rural France, all these are everyday meats. Try telling Cajuns they should not eat gator or native Australians they should not eat 'roo. Eating locally shot meat is normally one of the healthiest ways to source meat protein. Anthropomorphic naming of animals or their "Disneyfication" with human characteristics does not help those who then see them as fluffy bunnies or dewy-eyed fawns rather than a necessary meat source.

Peter's vision in Acts (10:9–16) means that we can rethink our meat choices. But how far? Remembering Singapore's Bugis Street food stalls, as I do from over thirty years ago, is still distressing, with its cages of live cramped birds and poultry, tethered primates as well as cats and dogs all awaiting the cook's knife. West African markets with their fly-covered shawls of bush meat, including severed great-ape limbs, is a sight to goad the conscience towards change.

Why are Ethical Meat-Eaters Necessary?

As we have read the preceding paragraphs, we may have recognized the importance of determining the ethics of our meat-eating or vegetarian choice. The simple answer that we eat meat because we like it is obviously inadequate. Tigers and pet dogs like meat. Thinking people need to have examined the arguments for and against eating meat. Some will choose to become vegetarian and some vegan.[2] Others will continue to eat meat. But why? And with how many questions?

So—unless we all choose to go vegan, therefore also foregoing animal products such as milk, cheese, and eggs in our diet—animals will need to be born and raised for human consumption. The arguments of this chapter affect vegetarians and pescatarians just as much as they do full meat-eaters. This chapter focuses on the meat-or-not issues; we return to the fishy questions in chapter 11.

This chapter's opening few paragraphs tell us that Christians either choose to have a wide-ranging protein diet as Jesus did or use other criteria for limiting their spectrum of nourishment. This chapter explores the four

2. Moules, *Fingerprints*.

broad philosophical "discussions" about meat consumption, while linking these to our faith questions.

The Climate Argument

In popular UK journalism, it is often said that Britain's dairy industry contributes more to global warming than the private UK use of motor vehicles. The very fact that this argument has not been loudly disproved or regularly shouted down shows it contains a significant measure of truth. All cattle produce methane gas, which in excess damages the atmosphere's ozone layer.

Any form of dairy product requires milk, from post-birth lactation, and this will inevitably produce surplus animals. Male calves (cattle or camels), goat kids, and male lambs can be castrated and raised for meat (or sold as pet food). If we want to have milk or any dairy products (cheese, yoghurt, butter, etc.), lactating cows will continue to be necessary, producing a surplus of bull-calves. "Dominion" will have its consequences, often involving compromises.

It is unrealistic to think that the Western world will move to a dairy-free diet. Many Inuit tribesmen use some reindeer milk in their predominantly meat-based diet. Milking sheep, goats, reindeer, or camels is a labor-intensive task. If we are to retain the significant use of milk, cheese, and other dairy products in Western-style diets, cattle will be utilized, and some meat production is a natural by-product. Despite having many vegetarian friends, I have not yet encountered a viable "vegetarian solution" to this conundrum.

This climate consideration is one half of the so-called "eco-argument" about the level of our meat production and consumption.

Meat Requires Too Much Planet

This is the other half of the "eco-argument."

All farmers know that it takes ten times as much grain or vegetable feed to produce the same weight in meat. In other words, 10 kg of grain produces only 1 kg of meat, approximately.

How many people can you feed with a 10 kg sack of grain and how many can you feed with 1 kg of meat? There is a vast difference. Essentially, the more grain we produce, the more people can be fed. The amount of grain it takes to produce your weekend burger can keep a family of four alive in sub-Saharan Africa for two days. How many people starve while you visit a drive-in burger house?

Remembering Charles Elliott's thinking, as well as this "10 kg : 1 kg" food ratio, every individual needs to question how often they can responsibly eat meat. This other half of the so-called "eco-argument" questions us about the level of our meat production and consumption. For several of my friends, this has led them to vegetarianism in the belief that more of the world will be fed if we all eat less meat.

However (and there is a big however), turning all our grazing land over to continual grain production is a "dustbowl practice"—see chapter 3. Clearly, crop rotation is vital, involving brassicas and root crops, even if labor-intensive, to avoid soil degradation. Scrubby ranchland may not be suitable for crop-growing but could be used to raise the dairy industry's beef animals.

That works in the USA where slaughtered carcasses can be chill-railroaded from the Midwest to the metropolitan meat markets. But in Britain, raising "hill-beef" is a dying farm practice and beef animals are now usually raised indoors or on the best lowland pasture. These practices create "food miles," which the US railroading avoids far more efficiently. In France, where there is more per capita land, beef can be raised in a variety of practices, slaughtered, and eaten locally. In Denmark, fewer beef or dual-purpose cattle are raised; so much of their beef has to be imported, creating both more food miles and a greater reliance on their domestic pork and poultry.

In the West, we have got used to the dollar-burger and inexpensive supermarket meat. We often fail to ask what it really costs to put that portion on our plate, not just in monetary terms, or even planetary ones. But for us to have our choice and plenty, who might be paying with their lives? If we want too many gas-producing cattle, that could include us—and not just those presently starving and crying out for grain.

Too Much Meat Damages the World's Health—and Yours!

The 2012 University of Chicago report, summarizing a twenty-year study, confirmed that too much red meat damages your health. A complementary Australian study confirmed that insufficient red meat can cause depression among women, because without other balancing dietary input, there *can* be a lack of the necessary antidepressant chemicals in the female bodily system.

As in the mid-1960s, with the first tobacco-causes-cancer reports, we have enough medical opinion (in 2013) to confirm that regular consumption of heavily processed meat products (such as sausages, brine-filled ham, processed meats, burgers, nuggets, and swizzles) causes bowel problems, including cancer.

This is a battle won but not the war. It will take another few such reports during a generation of Western bowel cancers to cause individuals and governments to ensure that meat-eating habits change. The amount of red meat consumed in China has incrementally soared since it became a BRIC economy. In 1960 the Chinese ate an average of less than 4 kg of meat per person per year; the World Health Organization's projections are that by 2010, that average had risen tenfold to nearly 40 kg per person. Perhaps a per capita survey of the incidence of Chinese bowel cancers pre-1970 compared with post-2010 will produce the damning evidence.

Shifting public opinion globally will be difficult. Jamie Oliver, another UK TV chef, won another debate to reduce such cheap and processed meats in school dinners, only to find some parents clamoring for their return. Are those parents guilty of some kind of child abuse?

My electrician raises organic free-range pigs and poultry on his edge-of-town smallholding. His home-produced sausages are so meaty, with little cereal content, that you need only one sausage on your plate to every three or four mass-produced (even "best quality" supermarket) sausages. This actually makes his meat portion cheaper than the mass-produced version. So one eats less, therefore eating more healthily. Sadly, I do know of teenagers and families who have become so used to eating cheap sausage that they choose against such organic goodies because they are "too meaty."

Working alongside a hospital dietician reminded me that the size of the ideal meat portion is about 50 g/2 oz—the size of a standard deck of cards. That amount is needed only three or four times per week at maximum. Consider this portion in relation to your Friday-night steak or your Sunday roast dinner.

Westernized meat consumption affects the planet, denies grain resources to the starving, and can damage individual health. Change is necessary.

The Animal Welfare Factor

In the preceding chapters, we have already explored the fact that the Hebrew and Christian traditions both need to interpret the biblical injunction that humankind has "dominion" over animals. The limits of such "dominion" have numerous outworkings. Can we apply Peter's vision to Bugis Street or the African bush-meat trade? My answer is no, but we have to lead the way in modeling exemplary practice.

Logically, if humankind wants dairy products, surplus meat animals occur. This creates the demand for butchery, which requires slaughter. That in its turn means that we should question how animals are kept and slaughtered for our needs. If we intend to keep domesticated livestock for meat, the divine "kill and eat" needs to be humane and appropriate. We return to the slaughter issues below.

The "animal welfare" argument is one of several points[3] that thinking people must respond to in either defending or maintaining their meat consumption.

Could You Slaughter Your Own Dinner?

I am a believer in the fact that you do not have to fall off a cliff to know it hurts. Have you asked how and why most gynecologists happen to be men (who never experience the intimate use of a speculum or giving birth)? I am not advocating that everyone must learn and experience how to wring a chicken's neck, use a humane killer, or slaughter their own food. But I do believe that you should know what happens to put meat on your plate.

After a heavy day's traveling in East Asia, our group stopped at a roadside stall and together ordered goat curry. Two struggling goats were brought for our choice before one was crudely dispatched with an axe. One of us has never eaten meat since that evening. After our shocked discussion, the rest of us decided to honor that goat's life by eating our fill, ensuring that all leftovers were given to our drivers and the street beggars. "Dominion" implies responsibility that the eater should have for the meat-providing animal, not to waste anything in giving up its life for our plates and palate.

There is no excuse for causing any innocent animal to suffer. As a teenager, I worked some shifts at a local slaughterhouse. Calmness and quiet are part of the atmosphere of a well-run abattoir. Animals do not need to be

3. The twin eco-discussions of "climate argument" and "Meat requires too much planet," the "health" and the "animal welfare" (including slaughter) issues.

panicked—in any case the chemicals so released can taint their flesh, and therefore the meat they produce. UK slaughter methods are well-regulated, demand pre-stunning, and, done properly, the animal knows nothing of what is happening except that it is in unfamiliar surroundings. . . . Is this society's "dominion"? If so regulation, inspection, hygiene, and care must be at the best levels.

I used to visit Joe regularly, who would often pick up one of his chickens at random to scratch its head, so that they all followed him around the yard. On some days, a bird was carried peacefully a little further, out of sight of the others, and its unsuspecting neck was broken in one quick movement. In both West Wales with John, and with Jeannot in France, we have walked a pig across a familiar yard; it was shot as it walked into the barn before being hauled up to bleed. I can reconcile these two examples of calm familiarity as humankind having "dominion" over creatures well-kept and killed.

I have witnessed regulated *halal* slaughter in Sparkbrook, Birmingham, and, alongside my East Asian or North African experiences, realize that these UK and global examples are worlds apart in standards of animal welfare. I have seen *shechita* or kosher slaughter in a Leeds abattoir and Israel, with nothing to divide them. Yet my Western philosophical sensibilities still prefer pre-stunning and/or home-killing of our food. I am not alone in that the European Union outlaws non-stun slaughter (except for religious communities' own consumption) and the British Veterinary Association has spoken out against both *shechita* and *halal* slaughter.

The UK *Sunday Times* reported[4] that, despite only 4.6 percent of Britain's population being Muslim and therefore requiring *halal* slaughter, nearly 50 percent of the UK's lamb in 2011 was *halal* slaughtered. Christian adults need to know what happened to their Sunday roast between the farm and the kitchen, and then to make sensible global decisions about how much they will actually eat. It is issues like these that make this particular discussion part of the "animal welfare" argument.

Fair Game

To be frank, wild field game that has been properly stalked and shot defeats all the moral arguments about the domestic raising and slaughter of meat animals. I have learned that from working with ghillies who were culling

4. September 30, 2012.

red deer in the Scottish highlands as well as with designated huntsmen who control fast-rising populations of wild boar in both the Ashdown Forest and the Forest of Dean, either side of southern England. Acquaintances say the same is true when dealing with southern Stateside and Australasian feral pigs.

Game birds, raised to live wild until the day of the shoot, that are properly shot from the air, know nothing of the panic of crated poultry on their way to the abattoir. Every country allotmenteer knows the need for the local rabbit population to be checked by a local 0.22 marksman.

To witness similar accuracy in the cull of feral camels in Australia or of surplus eland, gnu, or zebra in southern Africa is a reminder that meat so obtained is a food resource. It is as globally irresponsible to not use that wild food source as to leave much of one's meat portion on the side of the plate.

It is only those vegetarians who reject meat on the grounds of taste and/or texture, who can ethically choose to say that wild-killed game should not be a supplement to their own diets. The rest of us may as well enjoy wild game with greater relish than the Israelites did with the quail that arrived alongside the "manna in the wilderness" (Exod 16–17).

Insects

I have eaten wok-fried locusts, enjoying both crunch and taste. Across the world, over eighteen thousand varieties of insect are eaten. Whether it is pan-fried insect mixtures in Thailand or skewered scorpion kebabs in China, it all looks incredibly tasty; served with a vegetable sauce and rice they become a balanced meal. Consider how small a free-range space with either overripe fruit or some aging meat is needed to encourage insects to thrive and breed in profusion. The fact that it only needs 1.7–1.9 kg of meat or fruit product to produce 1 kg of insect protein means that such insect proteins can be far more efficiently produced than mammalian protein, which requires 10 kg of grain to produce 1 kg of meat. Is this part of the answer to the world's protein crisis? Across Westernized capital cities and metropolitan areas, restaurants are opening, offering specialist insect-based menus. However, I continue to balk at eating mealworm quiche![5]

---

5. *Sunday Times*, November 11, 2011.

What Should Happen . . . ?

The price of meat should rise significantly. The nature of the world's demands must push up the price of hill-raised beef, lamb, and *cheval*. Such free-range principles need to be applied to pork production too. Chicken and rabbit can be kept and surplus-produced by almost every small (and even urban) farmer.

Just over 10 percent of the British population is vegetarian, according to repeated articles in the Vegetarian Society's house journal. That is more people than watch professional sport (football, rugby) each weekend or weekly celebrate their faith in a church, mosque, temple, or synagogue. Vegetarianism is not for cranks but a lifestyle of choice. If we are vegetarians who enjoy dairy products, we are also complicit in the meat trade but we can ensure that the "logically occurring" meat, as the dairy by-product, is properly used as a matter of global responsibility. In the midst of the European "horse-meat scandal," Sir Paul McCartney (the former Beatle) was often interviewed about his thirty-year-plus life as a vegetarian and outlined the arguments of this chapter repeatedly that "change must happen."

Basically, if we choose to have meat in our diets, we should eat less of it, ensuring that it is high-quality, free-range, and organically produced as well as ethically "dispatched" in terms of food miles, slaughter, and sale. A "whole earth lifestyle" pushes us towards eating less meat but accepting it is better to pay more for higher-quality meat from known and local producers.

Personally, I have to recognize that my love for quality bacon sandwiches and turkey at Thanksgiving or Christmas, alongside duck, game, and rabbit, means that I choose to remain a meat-eater, but one who has to make responsible choices about where and how to shop or shoot.

8

Cereal Killers and Genetic Modification

During a "responsible eating" conference, I stayed with the family of one of the organizers. At Saturday breakfast time, the children rushed downstairs chattering about their weekend cereals. Their mom put out a set of packets of well-known (across three continents) brands and the kids filled their bowls. As we ate and talked, I noticed that on two of the cereal packets, there was something seriously wrong. The salt and sugar contents of an adult portion were respectively more than and equal to a child's daily prescribed intake. Eaten daily, those branded breakfast cereals are killers.

These parents knew that—which was why their kids could only have those cereals at weekends; oatmeal porridge year-round was their weekday breakfast. It says much that these responsible parents had checked that and worked out a system so their family did not feel disadvantaged among their peers.

Returning home, I took my clipboard down two different supermarkets' aisles and confirmed horrible truths. Many well-known breakfast cereals provide some significant majority, if not the total or more, of prescribed daily adult allowance of salt, various vitamins (or their substitutes!), and sugar in a single bowl. Do we not eat more salt, vitamins, and sugar at other meals? The threat of legal action means names of brands and cereal types cannot be published but I urge you to undertake a similar check of your family's favorite cereals.

Maize is the world's most produced staple cereal, followed by rice, then wheat; potato is the fourth most used carbohydrate "filler" globally, followed in fifth place by sorghum. When we consider that, we can recognize there is a problem. Sugar, salt, and flavorings all form part of schoolyard or supper cereal snacks such as crisps/chips, biscuits, pizzas, tacos, etc. The 2007 UK government figures stated that 75 percent of the salt we eat is already in the food we buy.[1] Think of your household's daily foodstuffs, then start reading the daily amounts of sugar and salt in so much of our grazing lifestyle.

The Tide of Diabetes

Diabetes is a medical condition in which the body does not produce enough insulin to "process" the intake of sugar. Clinically untreated, someone will die quickly as the condition worsens. If treated, even with daily monitoring and medication, it still creates long-term health risks of blindness, organ failure, cardiac complications, ulceration, and potential limb amputation.

Type 1 diabetes normally develops within childhood because the body's immune system closes down the natural system of insulin production. The costs of long-term treatment have to be borne by society-at-large via health insurance schemes or government funding.

The explosive problem is Type 2 diabetes. This is caused by overconsumption of sugar, exacerbated by (over)weight gain, excess alcohol, and ancillary health problems. Treating Type 2 diabetes in Western societies is both an economic and a social time bomb.

In 2012, the UK's *Journal of Diabetic Medicine* reported that treating diabetes cost £9.6 bn in 2010–11 with approximately 75 percent-plus of this figure for Type 2. Much of this cost would have been avoidable if adults had chosen and been given a healthy, low-sugar diet since childhood. This cost was then 10 percent of the total UK National Health Service budget. Frighteningly the projection of treating diabetes in 2035–36 will be just under £17 bn or one sixth of the National Health Service costs—and that is at today's prices.

Twenty-five percent of the UK population is now clinically classified as obese. In the USA, this figure rises to over 30 percent. In the UK, one in three meals consumed is a "ready meal" TV dinner. In the USA, one in three meals are consumed either as takeaways or in diners/luncheonettes, before anyone starts counting TV dinners.

Sadly, the USA presents an even bleaker scenario than these facts suggest. Exact figures are hard to discover because of different recording

---

1. UK Food Standards Agency, *The Little Book of Salt.*

practices, the greater use of generic, cheaper treatments, and the fact that healthcare costs (if privately, as against federally, funded) are not so publicized. In 2012, one in five adults had or will have some form of developing diabetic problem ultimately requiring costly long-term or acute treatment. But because of rising obesity, there is a health insurance expectation that this diabetic proportion could easily reach one in four US adults within a generation.

Diabetes and obesity will become Western society's biggest serial killers, both numerically and proportionately. Even addressing that problem with today's generation of children will still leave a big intermediate cost and problem. But the questions for parents is: would you knowingly give your children something every day that, in its overconsumption, will cause major threat to their long-term health? Again, remember that Jesus asked the question, "What manner of father would give his son a stone when he asks for bread, or a snake when he asks for a fish?"

Although this chapter is headed "*cereal killers*," we need to apply the same standards of check and restraints with both our canned and bottled goods. Driving home recently, I received a text message inviting me to a friend's for supper. As afterwards I washed up the just-emptied jar of pasta sauce, I realized that we had each eaten the equivalent of three large spoons of sugar in that one meal. To paraphrase the Bible, "in everything, be vigilant." In 2014 in the UK, national medical watchdogs, healthcare professional bodies, and politicians are beginning to have a much-reported debate about whether the UK needs to have a "sugar tax," imposed proportionately-or-not on all food products containing white sugar, from sodas through breakfast cereals, confectionery, and cooking sauces to "ready meals."

Healthy eating begins at home—but that begins with good research before and while we shop. This book is being sold throughout Western-oriented and affluent countries where people can make choices about what to buy—whether books or food—and what to eat. But not everyone has that choice, so we need to produce more food that enhances life rather than potentially damages our health.

The Genetically Modified Crops Debate

Genetic modification (GM) is the introduction of a gene from another organism (plant-to-plant, animal-to-animal) to strengthen the qualities or improve the yield of the host organism. The attitude to "genetically modified" crops varies significantly across the world.

For many years, the majority of Sicilian *Sanguinella* "blood oranges" sold in Britain have been genetically modified. These oranges are high in vitamin C, and other key chemicals, vital in combating both forms of diabetes, some cancers, and cardiac disease.

A Global and Ethical Dilemma

The way ethicists and biologists address particular issues varies from continent to continent. For instance, in the USA GM is forbidden but "stemcell" research is allowed, whereas in the UK the reverse is true. The UK is still in the midst of a huge ethical debate about whether stem-cell research should be further allowed beyond strictly licensed pilot situations. Yet UK government-funded plant research agencies are allowed to produce both laboratory and field-experimental GM crops. For theologians and ethicists, the nub issue in both stem-cell and GM is that this is human interference in the naturally evolved biological status of the host organism—whether plant or animal. GM and stem-cell research are two sides of a single ethical coin: what price are we prepared to pay for risking research into scientific processes that can create mutation?

Seeds, Subversives, and Spreading

Every year, I get my seed catalogues and pore over them. My high school biology means I know what an "f1 hybrid" variety is, but I cannot know whether they are GM because UK legislation does not force the sellers of seed to say so. Yet I also know that as far back as the 1990s, Britain was allowing the GM development of "flavor-saver" tomatoes. A subversive gardener-acquaintance ate his home-grown GM flavor-saver tomato-and-cheese sandwiches on the flight to work-stay with friends on their US Smoky Mountains smallholding, with its composting outhouse. Human excrement is a great medium for growing tomatoes, because they naturally germinate within it, even if then you only use the fruit as next year's seed.

Whatever the state legislation is, gradually the global spread of GM crops will occur. GM can be used to make particular crops resistant to particular herbicides, pests, or disease. GM can also be used to enhance particular genetic characteristics, such as in flavor-saver tomatoes, by increasing certain aspects such as the level of a particular vitamin in each fruit, grain, or seed.

The development and testing of GM crops carries large risks, which must be well-assessed. Once trials have to be taken beyond laboratory and then greenhouse conditions, the risks rise because of rain irrigation, wind movement, and avian carriage. Often the presence of encircling buffer crops, which are often burnt or destroyed, is not enough. In 1999–2000, the USA discovered that sufficient GM contamination had occurred that more than 25 percent of the US rice export market was lost. An additional concern is that organic herbicides cannot destroy such aberrant plants because they are so G-modified as to be resistant.

In February 2014, the University of Georgia, Cornell University, and other US partners announced they had successfully (under strict license) genetically modified sorghum (as stated above, this is the fifth most important cereal crop worldwide) to enable it to be a perennial—that is a plant or crop that does not need to be sown annually. They also know that the techniques thus developed can now be applied to other cereals, such as maize, wheat, domestic rice, and sunflowers. By making these GM crops become disease- and herbicide-resistant their cost of production should fall significantly. This may appear very positive, but how long can such monocropping continue without destroying the soil's goodness? Once again, think of "the cotton dustbowl" from Steinbeck's *The Grapes of Wrath*.

Franken-foods

It is little surprise that I have read the phrase "Franken-foods" in popular magazines either side of the Atlantic, when referring to GM. Within the EU, there is tight regulation surrounding the development of GM foods. But however good the risk assessments are at the laboratory, licensed greenhouse, and test-field stage, there comes a moment when that crop gets into the hands of farmers and backyard-growers. When thousands, then millions, start eating GM foodstuffs, it may be only after years, decades, generations down the line that we *can* know whether such tinkering with the planet's design is for good or ill.

Along with many other growers, I enjoy growing, tasting, and serving different varieties of tomato. But did I know that purple or black variety was GM? Probably not. There is enough popular evidence of UK companies developing GM tomatoes, but how many others among my garden crops are also GM, without my knowledge?

The problem is that many millions are already eating GM products. GM soya beans are being produced by the hundreds of tons in South America, for milling and processing into animal feed for cattle, pig, and poultry food. This is then imported into Britain, the EU, or North America, either directly as animal feed or as already processed burgers; if you live in the northern hemisphere, you have eaten GM. The arrival of Monsanto's GM soya bean plantations, replacing vast acreage of Atlantic Forest in both Paraguay and Brazil, has allowed spraying with Monsanto's herbicide. This leaves their GM soya standing, but destroys nearly every other form of plant life, before running back into the ocean—at what long-term cost?

What if GM wheat or maize or tomatoes, several generations onward, produces some as-yet-unknown detrimental side effect? Will it become a different kind of cereal killer?

In posing the question, "What in God's name are we eating?" we need to be prepared to sharpen the academic debate, just as much as lobbying for commercial regulation, as well as discussing the issues among family and friends. Four key questions are:

- What are the benefits?
- Who are the benefits for?
- Are those who are lobbying for change or relaxation, the very people who will increase their market share?
- Will this be a single-herbicide-repellent crop? A crop that is multi-herbicide-repellent is dangerous if it mutates into a fast-spreading, therefore uncontrollable, pest.

Part of the issue is that in the Western world only 2 percent of the population are actively involved with food production but 100 percent are involved in its consumption. The food production lobby and their concerns are small when compared to the general population.

Just north of London (in Hertfordshire), field trials of GM spring wheat are ongoing. This crop has been modified with a pheromone that resists the aphids that normally consume at least 20 percent of the wheat. Until something goes wrong, it can be assumed that a 95 percent plus yield can be expected, which is of both agricultural benefit and financial profit to the producer. As I write, this is not yet in commercial production. Now, I do share the concerns of other local growers, ethicists, and pressure groups (e.g., "Take the Flour Back") who are questioning the wisdom of this situation, but the toothpaste is out of the tube (you cannot put it back). The debate and lobbying now must focus on licensed-production farms and a statutorily required labeling policy—in similar style to that we now endorse on cigarette packaging. When UK hotels advertise that their kitchens use no GM crops, it suggests the concerns are widespread. In May 2012, the BBC broadcast across Europe a program summarizing the concerns about GM. In turn, other consequent programs were broadcast as listeners engaged both the BBC and popular newspapers in correspondence about the subject: another indicator of widespread questioning and concern.

"Let Me Have Apples with Spots On"

But the argument is not clear-cut. The world must heed the lessons of East Africa, which now suffers the long-term effects of the DDT used to kill off insects spreading lethal disease or devouring swathes of subsistence food crops. Since DDT's widespread usage, scientists have discovered that it also has devastating repercussions, in weakening both mammalian immune systems and avian egg shells, causing the loss of vital and necessary species from the natural food chain.

But just a few hundred miles north of the East African region, thousands still die in the Horn of Africa for lack of clean water and reasonable nutrition. This region was the target for 1985's Live Aid, in both the USA and the UK, and their successor concerts. Without caricature, most folks in the Horn of Africa can do much better than simply survive if there is enough cereal crop and enough clean water to provide mealie-porridge for all. But this requires action on several fronts, such as to provide clean water as well as hardy grain crops, which in turn create moral choices between either pest control or GM. Chemical pest control requires just as much monitoring, if not legislative restriction, as GM if mistakes are not to be repeated.

To improve cereal production, growers need to improve the nitrogen-fixation. The best way is to utilize plant strains which can "fix" molecular di-nitrogen. The world can already do this with legumes, like peas and beans. There is no way to shift this nitrogen-fixing character to cereal crops except by GM because it is important to breed across sufficiently different species.

Of course, there are benefits of GM. It can create climate-hardy so-called "supercrops" that are resistant to disease and drought, as well as providing longer-lasting, higher-yielding crops with less human and mechanical input.

If we truly believe that the world should be fed, we have to find a way to develop greater cereal production so that the starving too may share in Jesus' "life in all its fullness" (John 10:10). My Anabaptist-Mennonite theology means that "life in all its fullness" thinking must be directly applied to earthly priorities for all now and not just to some future heavenly realm. The alternative is that the "rest in the West" eat significantly less. However, the politics and expectation of that are generally unrealistic.

The Meat Debate Returns

The globally reported horse-meat-in-beefburgers scandal, first referred to in chapter 2, raises the specter of GM proteins. What appears to have also occurred is that horse-meat concentrates were "replicated," to quote a UK food minister, to become part of an ultra-cheap "protein powder additive." This substance was then exported back to the Irish meat-processing plant as the additional bulk for cheap, supermarket beefburgers for sale in the UK. What is important to stress in this example is that there may have been no genetic manipulation but simply the exercise of a food scam, which could be detected only by DNA testing.

The work of a Scottish university, Edinburgh's globally reported cloning of Dolly the sheep shows that GM of the meat supply chain is now feasible. This book has already highlighted the selective breeding of the more "meat efficient" Meidan pig. Imagine the effect if GM was significantly used to improve the nature of our meat-producing animals.

This chapter's emphasis is on how physiology (mal-)adapts. Whether that is internally within people (to create a dysfunctional physiology, such as diabetic-related conditions) or in the genetic medication of plants or animals, it still points to the fact that Western demands for a diet of what-we-want has become something commercial producers seek to fulfill—without ethically questioning what is good for the consumers, the customers, the producers.

Cheap meats often have an excess of sugar, salt, and cereals added to them, alongside injected water, to enhance both their bulk and their supposed taste. Cereal killers are not only in the packet at breakfast but in the ready meal or in budget-produced meat. Questioning our diet means reviewing the whole of what we eat.

If we are people of faith, there may be scriptural prohibitions of certain foods, such as in Judaism or Islam. Recently, I was talking with a UK imam who exhorts his congregation during Ramadan—a time of holy daylight fasting—to consider how they break that fast after dark, to be ever mindful of their less-fortunate brothers and sisters. His brother, another imam in France, reminds his congregation that the *hajj*, the holy pilgrimages to Mecca, is also a time to learn how to share bread with their sisters and brothers. If only Christian pastors and preachers would see such teaching as part of discipleship's agenda. Again recently, I was talking with a local UK doctor in general practice in a 90 percent Muslim neighborhood, who told me that about 80 percent of the diabetics registered at his surgery are white British who would claim they are Christians, or from that heritage.

What in God's name are we eating? And at whose expense?

In Conclusion

GM is a fact of life in Britain, Europe, and much of Australasia. Used well, it could help the world to move towards more adequately feeding everyone. The faith lobby is huge worldwide, therefore rightly taught and encouraged it could ensure appropriate legislative controls to enable global change. But this requires informed ethical debate in each Western nation as it recognizes its disproportionate share of the world's food resources.

I make no apology for writing a relatively technical chapter. Basic biochemistry teaches us that the natural starches in grain crops, rice, and potatoes convert into sugar. An excess of those starches naturally produces an excess of sugars. This excess is not good for long-term human health. Such cereal serial killers abound in the diets of Western societies.

The GM debate globally is like the US "gun control" debate. Wrongly used, GM and guns can bring death on a massive scale. Rightly used, guns can provide food humanely. Rightly used, GM can lead to better health for more of the world. The key issue is "control," and therefore who pulls the trigger—big business or the starving millions?

9

Free Trade, Fair Trade, Fair Prices, Fare Labels

THIS BOOK WILL HAVE revealed my love of traveling, rather than being a
tourist. I enjoy meeting local people, farmers, and sellers more than simply
the stallholders in tourist markets.

Years ago, when I used to take student groups to Taizé (the ecumenical monastery) in Burgundy, France, we used to travel by minibus and go
somewhere off the beaten track for another week, buying fresh food from
local markets. I have enjoyed eating at local shepherds' tables, during backpacking trips through the Greek islands and in the Scottish highlands. In
France, Scandinavia, and North America, I have gone to the local farmers'
(literally) market and bought all the food we needed for the weekend—
direct from each food's producer. Fewer food miles, fresh, mostly organic
produce, and an opportunity to talk with the grower, farmer, even slaugh-
terer; it sounds like the "principles" shopping list from this section of the
book.

However, very few of us can permanently live within such a producers'
market locality. Many of us are coerced by professional demands into cities
or at least urban sprawl. In such areas, there may be a "farmers' market" but
it is often so small that you cannot even buy all the main food groups there.
Because of bulk-buying, therefore lower retail prices, supermarkets have
pushed local shops into insolvency or out of business. In many ways, this
latter scenario is a microcosm of the vast majority of international trade.

The power of the conglomerate or multinational company to move its
purchasing power and production to wherever the cheapest cost may be

enforced nearly always removes rights and income from the producer and their workforce.

This principle and issue must concern us if we are concerned to have greater opportunity to determine the nature of our and others' diets, as well as care for our food producers.

Free Trade

Governments, multinational food conglomerates, and supermarkets use "free trade" as a mantra when very few of them actually really believe in it.

"Free trade" purports to say there is a level playing field and anyone can join in, assuming it will be for the market—that is, the consumers—to buy whatever they want at the best price. For most consumers this will be getting the best balance between cheapness and quality. But if you are poor, or your choice becomes more limited because of lack of competition, "free trade" means nothing if there is but a single choice or a single purchasing point or if an exclusivist cartel pertains.

Supermarkets

Supermarkets require uniformity of product. Whether it is meat, apples, bread, vegetables, or whatever, they want each particular product to be of a standard size and shape. Not only does it make mechanized prepackaging or transportation easier, but also they claim that it is what the consumer wants, ignoring the fact that all non-standardized products are rejected and normally thrown away before a customer sees them. It also stifles our ability to recognize and choose what we want—I am quite happy with a lop-sided chicken, spots on apples, and odd-shaped vegetables that I wish to eat but that I don't grow myself.

Reference has already been made to the ways in which supermarkets can suppress prices to producers, whether dairy farmers or mass vegetable growers, in order both to maintain low consistent prices to the consumer and to maximize their profit margins. This leads to gangmaster-style subjugation of low-paid, often illegal, migrant workers, or slipshod cut-price production, which allows horse-meat or salmonella into our food chain. How long will it be until a supermarket is proven to have condoned illicit practice to maintain its market share and its profits?

We all need something-like-supermarkets where we can bulk-buy pasta, rice, toilet rolls, fruit juices, family toiletries, and so on. But we seriously have to question the "one stop shop" mentality that will force specialist food (and other) retailers out of business. Supermarkets operate cartels, whether overt or hidden, to their advantage and not ours nor the producers.

Multinational Food Conglomerates

Earlier in this book, I referred to the Nestlé baby milk scandal and ensuing international boycott of their products. In the end, every member of our then household carried a list of nine seemingly different brands with over fifty products, which we regularly consulted so that we could avoid buying those products. This was an eye-opener, because we realized how easily our lifestyle had fallen into the hands and the control of a multinational. We began to change things and actively began to make more of our own everyday foods, such as sauces, ketchups, jams, and pickles, and we began bottling more fruit and freezing more vegetables. We were fortunate to have the shelf-space, the time, and the freezers to do all this—but learned from the Amish to work together in times of glut to pick, prepare, bottle, or freeze. Not everyone has such support.

The multinational is here to stay—unless there is some global revolution and all the planes are downed, and how likely is that? But international economics will cause changes and shifts in their names, alliances, and products. Once Britain had a premier chocolate company called Cadbury, who after some generations formed an international partnership with Schweppes; in the end their commercial interests diverged and they divorced just in time for the US Hershey corporation to gobble up Cadbury. With each maneuver, the regional workforces were told, even legally assured, there would be no change. Yet despite Hershey's promises it has become cheaper for them to break any legal commitments and to change patterns of production.

The European horse-meat scandal has revealed the convoluted paths of international ownerships and common directorships. Now nearly all British poultry processing is controlled via proxy companies upward to multinationals in either Brazil or India, where legislation of employment rights or animal welfare are very different from UK standards.

Governments

For many years the European Union was colloquially known as the "Common Market." It was a protectionist area, controlling the import of products from outside it, with tariffs, quotas, and import taxes. This may sound horribly familiar to readers in the Australasian region or the USA, Canada, and Mexico. In each region, either the large individual government or the regional union could control how easily others could trade with them while protecting the interests and products of their own country. Often, they would make grandiose statements about this being "free trade" and allowing the market to determine what could be sold where. It was only "free trade" if you were favored or somehow within their circle of welcome.

Governments maintain that they believe in and prefer "free trade" options. In essence, their introduction of protectionist tariffs or regional subsidies is like playing American football when the home team are allowed ten extra blockers. As a Christian, I believe such long-term protectionism (as exercised by both the USA and the EU) is biblically unjust and therefore wrong. Such "free trade" protectionism may have limited value in helping kick-start regional/sub-continental markets, such as now occurring with the MINT economies.[1] But whether it is US, EU, BRIC, or MINT exclusive protectionism, this becomes wrong when it does not taper off to nil, thus depriving so-called Third World, less-developed nations from gaining footholds to sell their crops and products too.

Fair Trade

As world travel for many grew, so did the developed world's awareness of the poverty of many in other lands. Outside of the Gulf countries or dictatorships, many Muslim nations demonstrated a significant awareness of the poor in their midst where egalitarian styles of dress and their faith's demand to give alms (both food and money) meant that even the poorest traders and their families survived. It was the Western-styled or so-called Christian nations of the developed world who had a log to take out of their own eyes. The pressure for low prices for goods emanating from those less-developed nations meant that producers of *our* tea, *our* coffee, *our* rice, *our* bananas, and so forth were being subjugated into virtual slavery at subsistence levels.

---

1. Professor Jim O'Neill's acronym for the next penumbrous circle of developing world economies, namely Mexico, Indonesia, Nigeria, and Turkey, hence MINT.

In Britain, various Christian agencies, such as Traidcraft and later Tearcraft, came together to bulk-buy chocolate, recycled goods, crafts, then later tea and coffee, then rice and sugars at fair prices from the producers to give them a living wage. These were sold through local agents, gaining 10 percent commission, through churches, in charity shops, and at weekly market stalls; our household ran one! This practice was known as "fair trade."

Not quite simultaneously, globally thinking people got behind the Dutch-based company *Solidaridad*, and launched the first fairly trading label, "Max Havelaar," selling a Mexico-sourced coffee in Dutch supermarkets. Max Havelaar was a fictional hero who had mobilized opposition to the exploitation of coffee-growers in the Dutch colonies. The "Max Havelaar" ideal and brand quickly spread through mainland Europe and Scandinavia. In Britain and Ireland, it was known as the "Fairtrade Mark," while in the USA, Canada, Germany, and Japan, it was known as "Transfair." In the USA, I first encountered "Transfair" goods being sold within the Mennonite-inspired "10,000 Villages" stores, set up as a North American version of the UK's Traidcraft.

In 1992, the Fairtrade Foundation, a charity, was set up in the UK by Traidcraft, the then four leading development aid charities, and an umbrella women's organization.[2] To quote the foundation itself: "in 1997, Fairtrade Labeling Organization International (FLO) was established in Bonn, Germany to unite the labeling initiatives under one umbrella and establish worldwide standards and certification."

By 2006, the Fairtrade Certification Mark harmonization internationally was cohering rapidly with only "Transfair USA," "Transfair Canada," and "Max Havelaar Switzerland" still to converge. Thanks to the lobbying of Christians and others, Germany, the Netherlands, and UK have each made the largest number of Fairtrade strides.

Two UK supermarket chains, the Co-operative and Sainsbury's, have competed with each other to introduce, then sell only particular ranges of fairly traded goods; now both supermarkets' own brands of tea, coffee, and chocolate are only "fair trade" as are their coconuts, bananas, and an increasing range of fruit and other foodstuffs. Their competition has encouraged Tesco and Asda (the UK's two largest) supermarket chains to either sell or create their own fairly traded brands of teas and coffees. The list of products grows, so much so that all two hundred UK Marks & Spencer

2. The National Federation of Women's Institutes.

department stores now sell only Fairtrade (marked) drinks in their in-house cafés.

Since 2001 in the UK, once a town reaches a majority percentage of shops and cafés selling Fairtrade goods, it can become and declare itself a Fairtrade town; friends who have had to relocate for professional reasons have deliberately sought to live in a Fairtrade town. I recently wrote a reference for an engineer-acquaintance whose prospective company's request information proudly displayed the statement "We are a Fairtrade company." Cadbury's most popular chocolate bar now has 100 percent Fairtrade ingredients. The tide continues to rise.

Regrettably (to me), in late 2013, decisions were made to allow a differently colored Fair Trade logo to begin to appear from mid-2014, indicating that such marked products are "Fair Trade lite." This means that only the main ingredient or 60 percent-plus of the contents are fairly traded rather than all or 98 percent-plus of the original Fairtrade-marked products. The argument ran from some producers that they could not source all ingredients as "Fair Trade" but wanted to be as fairly trading as possible. I think that this will let some producers ignore most "Fair Trade" principles while allowing them to claim commercially that they "are doing their best." I believe it will lead to consumer confusion.

Use Your Loaf

There is a British expression, "Use your loaf," meaning think properly about what you are contemplating. The L-O-AF principle is used in the UK in two ways; the first is to encourage shoppers always to buy Local, Organic, and Animal-Friendly products. Its second and preferential use is to stand for Local, Organic, Animal-friendly, and Fairtrade goods.

Fair Prices

In my most recent decade of traveling, it seems that more thinking people, not just Christian believers, are easily persuaded that openly paying a fair price for a product is the preferable option. Most people recognize that a trader is someone's husband, mother, or son and likewise a stallholder is someone's wife, father, or daughter. Human nature may like a bargain but no one who really thinks about the supply chain wants to deny another person their proper living or provision for their children.

In our collective, we rarely purchase "buy one—get one free" offers unless we know we have a real immediate use for the second item or know that another friend can utilize it presently. One of our current issues is to lobby Fairtrade product wholesalers gently to create bigger packets of foods such as rice, sugar, and pasta, saving on packaging costs to make family-scale buying easier. Another opportunity is to use independent shops, such as butchers, fishmongers, bakers, and greengrocers, or local veggie-box (or CSA) schemes—see next chapter. In most large cities, you can join a local food cooperative where discounts of wholesale bulk-buying trickle down to the retail consumer; some churches are beginning to run such cooperatives, often with a delivery service.

To pay a fair price may mean paying more in the medium term. To try and eat the same products as before, when utilizing less processed and/or supermarket products, will be expensive if sourced independently. For couples and families simply to change their lifestyle and cook together rather than eat TV dinners saves money. To move gradually towards a "whole earth" diet—more of this later—will eventually save money, but you will still be able to buy Fairtrade and/or pay fair prices to others.

Fare Labels

Some years ago, Felicity Lawrence, the *Guardian* newspaper journalist, wrote a great book, *Not on the Label*,[3] which helpfully exposed and explained the general con of food labeling. That book had the space (which this one does not) to help you understand what you should know from the labels attached to your fare. Basically, any ingredient that is listed that you do not understand should make you question the product's nutritional worth. This also applies to bold cover phrases like "flavor-enhanced" or "water-based" or "lite" or "sweetened for taste" and so on. Take your time when shopping—and take misleading packets to the store managers and question them firmly.

Long before the horse-meat scandal, people were saying that we have only the producer's assurance for what it says on the tin or packet; that is fact. Perhaps, it will take a number of such regional scandals or health scares about particular foods to force governmental action to be stronger against rogue producers or retailers or misleading labeling. An alternative

---

3. Lawrence, *Not on the Label.*

interim may be that wise and thinking consumers adapt their own personal household diets to buy more judiciously.

And So . . .

I remain convinced that we are many years away from the tipping point when consumers alone can enforce change simply through alternative patterns of purchasing. However, the careful and successive lobbying for and consequent purchase of each new Fairtrade item has created a sustainable demand in both supermarkets and independent shops.

More clarity is needed in governmental policies about the trading tariffs, restrictions, and quotas just as there needs to be a standardized and simplified but national scheme of labeling to show every mass-produced foodstuff's nutritional worth. What in God's name are you eating? Can you really believe it is what it says it is? Do you know that its producer and their family will not go to bed hungry tonight?

10

Self-Sufficiency, Simplicity, and Grow Your Own

APART FROM PICKY TEENAGERS, nearly everyone enjoys freshly produced vegetables. Most of my summer guests like seeing how quickly I can get something from plot to plate—and appropriately prepared. A freshly picked, washed then chopped salad of red, yellow, and tiger-stripe tomatoes is a feast for the eye as well as the palate.

Recently, I saw a Discovery Channel TV program in which a Cajun trapper in Louisiana claimed to be self-sufficient. He spoke of trading "garfish and other swamp critters" for sacks of flour, bags of salt, and jars of coffee, as well as gas for his boat at the trading post. He was doing pretty well but he *is not* self-sufficient—he operates as part of a barter economy.

There is a Western myth that self-sufficiency exists; there is no such thing as self-sufficiency. Even Scottish Hebridean crofters, Pennsylvania Amish farmers, and rural Aboriginal Australians can no longer live in isolation from the economic pressures surrounding their lifestyles.

While *complete* self-sufficiency is impossible in the modern world, it would be very beneficial if many more of us moved in that direction. An increase in self-sufficiency may be something to aim towards in order to downshift and simplify one's lifestyle. Even in the breadth of climate of North America or Australasia, it is well-nigh impossible for a nation to be self-sufficient and hang on to its current lifestyle, however simple.

But even our Western sophistication is rooted in a past of subsistence farming, whether that is of Midwest sharecroppers, transported convicts' colonies, or medieval serfs. Whether the cause might be catastrophe, cataclysm, or revolution, we all need to question how good at producing our own food we could be if we had to get back to the land. Let's start with that . . .

Growing Your Own

When Western-nation growers visit East Asia, it is easy to be astounded by the local abundance.

- Driving across the mangrove swamps from Bali's airport, one sees peasant homes each with a hugely productive raised bed next to it and a surfeit of fallen pineapples from that family's trees.

- Take the bus across the Johore causeway from Malaysia to the more rural areas of Singapore and one is quickly surrounded by similar artisan homes, with a bamboo boundary frame used for growing vegetables vertically, some fruit trees, and a tabletop-sized duck pond full of quacking meat and potential eggs.

- In Borneo, the longhouses used to have enough slash-and-burn space for vegetable gardens and semi-feral pigs until Western industrial loggers restrained such expansive practice.

- In the Philippines, on Mindanao, the contrast between urban Manila's cosmopolitan growth and the produce in the just-out-of-town vegetable gardens of the poorest workers is marked.

This brief survey demonstrates that even with the advent of rapid urbanization, high-density populations, and long-working hours (apart from the rich) many folk "grow their own" as an extension of previous generations' form of subsistence farming; in the UK, this is known as "grow your own" (GYO).

Does Growing Your Own Mean Compromise?

These selective examples show that where climatic conditions allow and governments do not restrict, clear patterns of families producing much of their own varied diet can and does work.

- Weekending with a Swedish family at their Baltic-island home involved working a tennis-court-sized vegetable plot; its produce graced our table and surpluses went back to their Stockholm apartment on Sunday night.

- Another weekend, a close friend's Russian hosts took him to their somewhat basic dacha well out of Moscow, where they worked hard on the vegetable garden by day, then swam in a creek to cool off from the summer heat before drinking vodka into the night.

- One of my village neighbors in southwest France spent his weekends tending his beehives and a small vegetable plot before returning to work and his apartment in Bordeaux for the intervening working week.

Even urban Western life can be built around producing one's food without compromising a quality of life. These three examples show that even city apartment living need not reduce the potential for GYO.

A quick survey of Western-styled nations underpins that. In Britain, we have long-standing traditions of a family being able to low-rent a plot of growing land from their city, town, or local authority for the purposes of raising food. These plots are called allotments and are usually about one-twelfth of an acre (0.05 ha).

Spain and Italy also have a long-standing tradition of such small plots outside town; they are called *huertos*. Until its revolution, nearly all of Cuba's land was owned by 1 percent of the people; (whatever his faults) Castro restored land to the workers so there were 25,000 such *huertos* there by 1995. Dynamically, some Cuban villagers banded their land together to make *organoponicos,* or market gardens, growing crops for barter and local sale. Their success meant that the Cuban Government legislated in 1996 that all further food production must be organic. Hallelujah!

But over a century before, in Germany, the Schreber movement of 1865 successfully campaigned that every citizen should have a statutory right to rent some land *locally* for crop production for their family; that right remains today. Germany's example spread across the Baltic and national boundaries. It was in 1895 that Anna Lindhagen, a wealthy Swedish woman, wrote about enabling every Swedish family to grow most of their own vegetables. By 1921 a national organization of Swedish allotments was in existence to protect the rights of their "stewards" and now that federation reports there are 26,000 such formally delineated allotment-sites within towns and cities. Almost parallel to this was the 1916 beginning of allotment development in Denmark where, by World War II, there were

100,000 such garden plots. It says something of the Westernization of the Philippines that in 2003 they had to enshrine the right of grow-your-own allotments in law.

Again the examples of Western-European-styled countries demonstrates that a strong GYO culture continues even in densely populated countries. The key issues here are the protected provision of land for individual family usage and the desire of those families to grow at least some of their own food.

The British Experience

In Dickens' *Great Expectations*, Wemmick, the London legal clerk, raises a pig and grows vegetables in urban east London; that was common in the Victorian era. During World War II, the Dig for Victory campaign meant every available piece of land from folks' backyards to public parks were transformed as tired workers grew vegetables for home consumption. 1950's British *cinema verité* often showed the working man on his allotment, helping the growth of this movement.

When I first owned a downtown home in the 1970s, I easily gained tenure of an allotment but now (in another location) I have been on a waiting list for five years. This is a common UK experience and, across Britain, folk are beginning to share suburban gardens, church backyards, and community patches.[1] There has been an explosion of interest in GYO, partly driven by the desire for greater food-quality control and partly because of the global recession's rising costs.

Community-Supported Agriculture

There are many variations on the community-supported agriculture (CSA) idea. Basically, a group with a guaranteed lease on some land appoints coordinators who plan year-round vegetable production on behalf of all the shareholders. Normally each shareholder provides so much voluntary labor per month, receiving a regular (weekly, fortnightly, monthly) box of produce in return for underwriting their share of the costs.

These schemes are gradually discovering their British equivalent, having first become popular in North America (where they are often known as Community Supported Agriculture schemes) and temperate northern

1. *The Guardian*, September 3, 2011.

Europe; another kind of *organoponicos*. The first professionally organized model that I encountered is just outside Minneapolis, serving a village of seventy households, each of which pays US $500 per annum towards seeds, tools, and the market gardener who leads each household's monthly "day of labor" on the land; participants are now saying they are growing too much veg! On current exchange rates their financial commitment is equivalent to about £7 per week but, committed annually, for that they get a box three times the size of a medium veg box from our local UK supplier whose cheapest smaller box is £10 per week.

In Bristol (England), one such CSA scheme uses both the long-term unemployed and recovering psychiatric patients as extra labor, assisting in their rehabilitation as well as the scheme's productivity. While recognizing these are but two examples of CSA, I am convinced that the economic advantages stack up in favor of share-cropping.

I know of more informal schemes, such as one led by two Mennonite housewives for their Alsace-Lorraine village, and similarly sized British share-cropping groups near Stroud and Todmorden in England, and Stirling in Scotland. My perception is that small groups of allotmenteers or your own collective could start such a group on some redundant land close to home, providing good wholesome veg while building a stronger local community.

Simplicity

In prewar Germany and 1940s Paraguay, both Mennonite and Bruderhof communities pioneered a rediscovery of simplicity in the back-to-the-land movement. In 1960s California, the hippy movement utilized the likes of Lou Gottlieb's jazz music or Bill Wheeler's wealth to form free-access communes in self-built domes and tepees scattered among vegetable gardens. In 1970s Scotland, the coming together of the Findhorn community was predicated upon amazing organic vegetable production. The 1980s global rediscovery of the simplicity of the Amish lifestyle (in North America) and Moravian settlements (in the UK) caused many thinking folks to question the nature of a yuppie, financially driven society.

The 1990s witnessed the gradual fear of millennium meltdown leading many to reappraise their city lifestyles. Some created veg gardens and energy-efficient homes while others abandoned the rat race to find tranquility in the Rockies, the outback or the Welsh Marches, where many have stayed with simplified lifestyles and homes. This gave rise to the movement called "downshifting."[2]

The ongoing global recession from 2005 has caused many to question whether simplicity rather than sophistication will be the life-giving motivator. In the USA, the prevalence of "doomsday preppers," either stockpiling seed or preparing to "bug out" self-sufficiently, has given rise to television series.

This trajectory of seeking "alternatives" over more than the past half-century, in the face of sophisticated, complex urbanization, proves there is a desire for a simpler way of living. My continuing contact with folks representing each of these examples commonly identifies four things:

- A desire not to return to their quasi-independent, non-cooperative past life;

- A practical commitment to work whatever amount of land they are entrusted with;

- A need to rediscover an inner simplicity to "tread lightly upon the land" as thinking global citizens; and

- A decision to use less of the world's resources.

Simplicity of heart and lifestyle travel naturally together with a desire to be involved in one's own food production. Those who choose alternative lifestyles to the past norms are becoming the new pioneers. Simplicity is the choice of those who know that "enough is enough."[3]

My very English grandparents used to speak often about thrift and "saving for a rainy day." This was the norm of their generation, born at the end of the nineteenth century. One had to "make do and mend." They would be appalled at the throwaway nature of twenty-first-century society. Shoes, small electrical goods, and cooking pots were always repaired and not thrown away. They had lived through the privations and rationing of World War II, allowing "no waste on plates," making stock out of all meat or fish bones, and composting everything possible. In Wales, the Mellowcroft community has developed an organic eco-center with camping ground and meeting spaces where they teach downshifting practices and GYO. In the rediscovery of "make do and mend," "downshifting," and GYO values, there is real opportunity to reduce our overconsumption of earth's resources.

2. Ghazi and Jones, *Downshifting*.
3. Taylor, *Enough is Enough*.

Self-Sufficiency

To be fair to that Cajun trapper at this chapter's beginning, he is the equivalent of an anonymous "Crocodile Dundee"—the bushman who can live off the land. 1960s hippies did not survive without US (government-provided) commodities. Present-day Amish and Moravians still need the mall for a sizeable minority of their groceries. Unchecked urbanization is the extravagance of a lifestyle that creates greater dependence upon others for processed foodstuffs, unseasonal fruit and vegetables, and the desire for "more."

We "work" with a small collective of friends to share resources. We swap or give away our vegetable gluts. We make our own tomato and onion ketchups. One keeps bees, producing honey; others have chickens—their own or their neighbors'. Another makes great hedgerow wines from particular fruits or vegetables. We all are committed bread-makers—but occasionally buy loaves from artisan bakers, organic food shops, or farmers' markets. All of us have some vegetable plots and fruit trees. But what we enjoy is swapping and sharing our produce. We may not be self-sufficient but we realize that with a little more effort and land, we could easily take several more steps towards food self-sufficiency.

I have just watched a globally broadcast TV program about a vegan Englishman who grows all his own food on a well-gardened plot about the size of two tennis courts. When questioned about his self-sufficiency, he tapped his metal spade and pointed to his polytunnels and said, "I'm not."

For some years, I used to help a friend dispatch the latest crop of his urban-backyard-raised rabbit. Gradually, because of that meat's culinary versatility, the only other meats he and his family ever consumed were organic sausage, bacon, and their Christmas free-range turkey. Although they recognized that they could be self-sufficient in raising meat, they acknowledged that they still had to buy in pelleted food and hay for rabbit bedding.

Two individuals, particularly, have challenged the world's thinking about wholesale life change towards earth-friendlier lifestyles.

The first is John Seymour, an idiosyncratic Englishman, who moved through several stages of self-sufficiency via boats, farms, and a smallholding. He wrote the first definitive guide on the subject for modern-day Western Europe.[4] I attended a couple of Seymour's courses at his West Wales school before he moved to his last training farm in Ireland. Seymour encouraged the ongoing increase of personal food production, keeping (and

4. Seymour, *Self-Sufficiency*.

killing) relevant livestock, while acquiring more skills to build, grow, husband, etc. Although he produced both tools and many keen students of his methods, he was a barterer like the Cajun trapper, from specialist animal feed to salt, flour, and tea. Seymour helped ask the questions but he knew the answer for total self-sufficiency would require an apocalyptic upheaval from the acquisitive society.

At the other side of the world, a New Zealander, Bill Mollison, had far more chance of changing Western cultures. Mollison is regarded as the father of permaculture.[5] This is a system of no-dig intensive food production, by inter-cropping, multi-cropping, and good composting, while creating homes, gardens, and settlements that take the fullest advantage of climate and topography. The permaculture movement is transforming the world of domestic food production. Britain's Bob Flowerdew (often heard on BBC Radio 4's *Gardeners' Question Time*) is an exponent of its principles,[6] utilizing so much of society's junk (notably, old car tires) in which to produce food intensively.

Making the Connections . . .

Perhaps it requires a land shortage, high prices, and densely populated countries to force folks towards Vaclav Smil's analysis that we can produce our own food. Perhaps that is why many in the big countries of America and Australia do not undertake much backyard food production. Perhaps that is why you must make the connection and change your lifestyle eco-positively.

Let me encourage you. In midtown Los Angeles, Christopher and Dolores-Lynn Nyerges run courses from their home, with its livestock, fruit trees, bees, and veg patches, to help others grow their own food and live more eco-aware lives.[7] Equally, in Sydney, Australia, the Permaculture Education Unit has plans for transforming a standard quarter-acre garden into one geared for intensive domestic food production.[8] Such city examples in big countries, alongside East Asia's and Western Europe's garden plots, can be the encouragement that the world needs to GYO, producing

5. Mollison, *Permaculture.*
6. Flowerdew, *Organic Bible.*
7. Nyerges, *Extreme Simplicity.*
8. Mollison, *Introduction to Permaculture*, 211.

great-quality crops at low cost to people and the planet. "What in God's name are you eating?"—you can answer because you grew it.

11

The End of the Line . . .

THIS CHAPTER DRAWS TOGETHER many threads from the preceding ones. Christians have to recognize there comes a moment when things have to change. Some of our attitudes to "dominion" can be graphically illustrated by this chapter's subject: fish. There is a complementary, bigger aspect of "dominion," when we consider fish. How often have we walked along the shoreline and seen the huge amount of human waste and other detritus washed up by the tide?

So often humankind has treated the seas, which cover 70 percent of the earth's surface, as both a playground and a dumping ground, assuming the marine environment is big enough to absorb and process our pollution. This is "dominion" of the worst sort: humankind is not the Lord of creation. Equally, because we cannot count the fish in the sea, we just assume they are there until there is nothing in the net or on the end of our line. The overuse of the world's piscine resources will lead to breed extinctions, disruption of necessary marine food chains, and loss of a human food resource. Again this is "dominion" of the worst order.

As we consider what may be an appropriate twenty-first-century "Jesus-shaped diet" or "whole earth" diet, we need to recognize how we use the Bible. There is no escape from the Gospel evidence that Jesus befriended fishermen and ate fish himself. The consideration of fish as part of our diet, whatever our decision about quantity, is necessary. But how we use the biblical material has to reflect what we know in our present circumstance.

Let me offer two biblical examples:

- In biblical times, slavery was a common practice. In Genesis 37, we read of how Joseph was sold into slavery by his own brothers. Across the Hebrew Scriptures, we read of the abuse of slaves by their patriarchal masters. In the New Testament era, Paul's Letter to Philemon commending an alternative response (to branding or execution) for the runaway slave Onesimus tells that even among Christians slavery was not uncommon. Now in the third millennium, the UK, the USA, and the Western civilized world has outlawed the practice of slavery. It still goes on but no Christian would call for its practice or reintroduction.

- In biblical times, the subjugation of women was normative. The sexual abuse of women by Abraham, Jethro, and David, among many, is documented; the unquestioning acceptance of that today is wrongful chauvinism. The fears about the women as witnesses to Jesus' resurrection arose because they were not statutorily acceptable as witnesses. Is this why the gender of Cleopas' companion on the Emmaus Road is not mentioned? One does not have to be a feminist to accept that there can be a reasoned and academic construct showing that the Bible has been written from a male bias, which needs serious reflection and not outright rejection.

If we are to be Jesus-shaped disciples, we have to see ourselves as part of the cosmos of the eternal God's creation and not abusers of the planet and our common humanity. Times change. Scientific evidence is advanced beyond natural comprehension for those from biblical days. The world's population has doubled to virtually seven billion in my lifetime and the planet cannot simply absorb all that extra consumption. We need to be prepared to recognize, then act, upon the fact that some practices just cannot continue.

Fishing

Or should this section be entitled "overfishing"?

In North America, both reputable US and Canadian newspapers regularly run extended articles questioning the potential overfishing of Arctic waters, the Newfoundland fishing grounds, or Pacific shores. That readers digest these articles in the Midwest and landlocked provinces indicates there is a truth to be discussed even if the balance of the arguments is not yet resolved. For Steinbeck readers, the change in the fishing industry between the Monterey of *Cannery Row*[1] and today is stark.

A gradual tide of evidence, from folk memory and scientific analysts, shows that, in many matters of food policy, the world is nearing the end of the line.

North Americans need only recall the huge effort, energy, and economy required to bring back Lake Erie from its poisoned days to realize that once horrible facts are in our backyard, if not on our doorstep, we have to do something. Would anyone have really suggested not cleaning up the bayous and Gulf Coast after Hurricane Katrina, or Prince William Sound in 1989 after the *Exxon Valdez* disaster? It takes generations to realize the impacts of such things on underwater ecologies. How many of my North American friends would give up Canadian salmon or Louisiana shrimp as hors d'oeuvres at Thanksgiving or Christmas? To keep our treats, we have to be prepared to meet both the economic and ecological costs.

What the Eye Does Not See . . .

The obvious problem is that fish live underwater. Until some species stop appearing on the end of your line or in the trawlermen's nets, no one begins to take account of the ecological toll of overfishing. Having watched the work of an Australian fisheries patrol vessel, I realize maintaining healthy fish stocks is clearly a matter of care, political will, and federal finance.

In the European Union, one of the greatest causes for argument between constituent nations is that concerning fishing quotas. These demand that each nation's fishermen land a certain quota of particular fish, such as cod, haddock, plaice, and so on. In turn this means each fishing boat gets given an allocation that must not be exceeded. The fishermen either stop work once their quota is achieved or, ludicrously, have to start throwing already dead, but perfectly eatable, fish overboard. We have not yet invented nets that catch only particular fish species, and we never will! Why not work with more localized regional quotas and clearer delineation of which nations can fish where? Why not sell over-quota fish at a higher rate to the retail customer, utilizing the extra taxes so generated on fish stock preservation programs? Why not learn how to cook sustainable breeds of fish?[2]

---

1. Steinbeck, *Cannery Row.*
2. Van Olphem and Kime, *Fish Tales.*

Although this situation commonly prevails, Hugh Fearnley-Whittingstall, the UK-TV-chef-turned-food-campaigner, has been spearheading a campaign for this quota-system to drastically change for the better. Following a single 2012 networked TV program, Fearnley-Whittingstall enlisted the internet support of 650,000 Brits (over 1 percent of the UK population), and according to a February 2014 government statement, appears to have won the arguments so the government will now legislatively repeal this appallingly wasteful process.

Most thinking people, not just Christians, already know that the only tuna to buy, ethically speaking, has to be line-caught. Netting tuna causes havoc to other species, particularly smaller cetaceans like dolphins. If I want to serve salmon to friends, I want to know how it got to my fishmonger's slab. Was it line-caught, wild, or farmed? We have to be prepared to pay more for our fish portion if it is to be ethically harvested. In Britain, we are fortunate to have the Marine Conservation Society, which both provides guidelines about ethically caught fish and awards its MSC logo for its packaging accordingly.[3]

As a cook, I enjoy the challenge of using alternative kinds of fish. In many fish stews, pies, or other dishes, few Brits can tell the difference between cod and well-seasoned rock-salmon (dogfish); in a cookery book, I would offer many more alternatives. Many years ago, I was camping in the French Camargue next to a holidaying Parisian chef—together we made the famous bouillabaisse (chunky fish stew) with local fish bought in Aigues-Mortes at a fraction of their Paris prices. We need to think about using more locally produced fish in our diet *or* that which can still be profitably and economically sold after long-distance transportation.

Fish-Farming

We had been walking in the Black Cuillin mountains on the Scottish island of Skye. Walking towards our guesthouse on the shore of the sea-loch, we spotted tennis-court-sized fish enclosures floating some distance offshore. It turned out that wild salmon was being farmed in that tidal sea-loch.

Our guesthouse hostess told us the story of how this new industry was revitalizing their community. The investment had come from Ian Anderson, of the globally famous Jethro Tull rock group, who had provided employment for both Skyelanders and former members of his band's

3. www.fishonline.org

road-crew. The influx of employment and workers had saved village schools from closure, local shops from bankruptcy, and helped build new communities. Today that Strathaird salmon is sold by fine retailers across the UK and beyond.

In similar vein, Practical Action[4]—the Schumacher-oriented, UK-based, development charity—works with indigenous Bangladeshis to develop much smaller-scale fish farms. Bangladesh is a land prone to 50 percent-plus flooding annually. Practical Action donates to local villagers a one-meter cube made from bamboo and netting supported by floats, also stocking it with a breeding stock of edible fish. Increasingly enabling such small-scale sustainable enterprise using these *hapas* (as they are locally known) is creating employment, nourishment, and wealth for local villagers. Equally important, it is making the vital statement that sustainable enterprise for food production and income creation is not just possible but incremental.

These two disparate examples remind us that it is visionary investment that can create possibilities, bringing food production and economic development in local communities. Perhaps Jesus' teaching about "bigger barns" or having "two coats" should challenge Westernized Christian communities away from big building projects and flashy inward-looking programs into prophetic action towards furthering such visionary enterprise. Perhaps when others see Christians enabling Jesus' words, "that the world might have life," come to better practical reality, they will sit down, eat with us, and listen to more of the Jesus story.

Whaling[5]

It was a sunny Hebridean afternoon with a swelling sea when, about ten metres from our boat, a minke whale raised its head. It looked at us all, turning gently before diving. It rose up again, slightly further away with a companion. Both looked at us, then each other, "spouted," and were gone.

Whether one watches whales off the coast of California or in the southern oceans or in the Scottish Hebrides, we see social, relational fellow creatures of the cosmos. In a small boat, they will often surface close-by

4. www.practicalaction.org.

5. I do know that whales are mammals and not fish but this form of hunting is popularly referred to as fishing, hence its inclusion here.

and "eyeball" you. Immediately you recognize their sentience in that visual exchange.

I have seen killer whales, minkes, wild dolphins, and other species in the Hebrides, Moray Firth, Biscay, and the Mediterranean. Each time I become increasingly convinced that they are sentient creatures. Their eyes and movement tell of an intelligence (which one witnesses too in captive great apes or Rwanda's mountain gorillas). Humankind has not listened to research scientists who have spent years recognizing that sentience also. This is what makes whaling (the deliberate hunting of cetacean species for whatever purpose—food, research, or profit) such an atrocity.

Whether one agrees with *Sea Shepherd's* tactics or not, their globally broadcast television programs have brought home more about the horror of whaling, far more than Herman Melville or *Captain Courageous* has ever done.[6] There can be no excuse for incessantly chasing whales to exhaustion. To then fire a rocket harpoon into the guts of any sentient creature— where it explodes causing them to drown slowly and painfully in blood and brine—is cruel, wrong, and unacceptable. The fortunate whale drowns, the unfortunate whale is hauled, semi-conscious, for some distance until the coup de grâce is administered by a high-powered rifle. This is not "dominion," this is abject cruelty. The excuse of some civilized governments that this is for research is patently untrue.

If only some Christians knew how many whale by-products are used in some cosmetics, lipstick, and other products—but that's another book. However, we can all take a stance.

After speaking at a Christian day conference, my generous hosts took me to a sushi bar. As soon as I spotted whale-meat on the conveyor-stand, I asked that we leave immediately—but not until I had spoken to the manager, explaining how unacceptable this was. All their fellow church members now avoid and ask their friends to avoid that sushi bar. Until we start to make a stance, commercial constraints will be reckoned to outweigh the ethics of "dominion." Since then a number of London sushi bars have been statutorily cautioned or successfully prosecuted for selling whale meat.

Christians have to be prepared to make economic choices, while publicly campaigning so that change occurs. People never believed that slavery would end. It is a matter of general knowledge that the majority of whale

6 Cf. www.seashepherd.org, established internationally in 1977 by Paul Watson (one of the founders of Greenpeace) as an activist campaigning organization working to protect whales, dolphins, and other forms of marine life from cruel and unnecessary predations by humankind.

species are seriously endangered. I want our grandchildren to take their children whale-watching. Whaling needs to end now. No more discussion—just stop.

One major step on the way occurred in March 2014, when the Australian government won their case in the International Court of Justice, which ruled against Japan's continued whaling in the southern oceans. However, the Japanese government are still saying that they might either appeal against that decision or change their hunting grounds. Vigilance is still necessary.

Conclusion

People of faith believe the purposes of the cosmos and creation are intertwined as well as being interdependent. Whales and all cetaceans are mammals and not fish, yet so many folk just assume that all marine life is part of a different cosmos from our own, just because they are sea-dwelling. We treat marine life as a disposable commodity just as slaves were treated in biblical days. We know that change can occur.

We have now reached the end of the line. This chapter's subject tells us most starkly about this. Folks will continue to cut down rain forests to ranch beef for burgers or for palm-oil plantations until the world fries with global warming when there are not enough trees to process carbon dioxide. The political and marine-biological machinations rumble on; in September 2013, the MSC had to declare that European mackerel quotas must be further reduced because of overfishing, yet isolated fishing communities know they face economic disaster if such quotas are reduced.[7]

But today most Brits can no longer assume their traditional "fish and chips (a.k.a. fries) suppers" will feature cod, plaice, or haddock. What happens to the tourist economies of those Pacific seaboard towns or New Zealand coastal villages when no one comes anymore because there are no more whales to watch?

Overfishing has occurred. We are at the end of the line. Fresh visionary thinking is required. Farming Scottish salmon or tilapia (a large meaty fish) in the tropics or in *hapas*, if undertaken sustainably, can form part of a creative future vision. We can learn something from those Singaporean households with their tiny fishponds about how easily many households could produce fish protein for human consumption. Any serious

---

7. UK *Sunday Times* Business News, September 22, 2013.

permaculturist knows the importance of complementary fish production, whether in household ponds or swales (drainage canals).

This "fish" chapter so questions us that it brings us back continually to the wider sustainability debate. It shows what overconsumption does to North Atlantic fish stocks. It reveals our ability to make prophetic change either as individual entrepreneurs or charity donors. It reveals our inhumanity in not knowing when "enough is enough" and we have reached the end of the line.

After a morning's line-fishing in Cornwall, I catch enough mackerel and other edible fish not just for supper but for the next three months' supply for the freezer. Can I still justify this if commercial pelagic fishermen are prevented from fishing by legal quotas? I may eat everything I catch and the bones and fish-heads are turned into stock for soup, but one day there may be nothing on the end of the line unless globally we all take action now. This is not just about me, or even you, but about a world in which too many starve because we cannot learn how to share harvestable, sustainable protein.

PART FOUR

Changing the World

12

Start Here

How we begin to think about and then change our ways with food varies. For some, it begins simply with what is practical and/or what is affordable. Others begin with principles. Often many of us are influenced by our friends' attitudes or reactions, particularly when we are sharing meals or if we are cooking together. Think how many people you know who share recipes, talk about food, or cook together.

This section of the book contains fifty-seven practical suggestions. Not all can or will work for you and your household. The important point is that there are these possibilities in each of our societies and locations. I doubt whether any reader has put them all into practice yet.

1. Address Book

One of my most helpful aids is my food-supply address book. If either you, your partner, or local friends or family regularly travel for work, leisure, etc., it can be worth noting your network of suppliers. In these transitional days, it will take years to perfect a lifestyle that is totally reliant on locally produced food. But in the interim, for those of us in metropolitan areas or well-populated regions or smaller countries (like New Zealand or Britain), this can work well.

Often, with more distant suppliers, you can preorder goods for collection if time precludes a longer visit to choose what looks best on the day (keep a cool-box in the car trunk). One trick is to color-code a normal address book; I use highlighters—pink for butchers, blue for fishmongers, green for greengrocers and farm shops, yellow for wholefood stores and cheese suppliers, and orange for game merchants. Then remember to keep it in the car glove box . . . it is no good on your hallway shelf! You also need to keep the suppliers listed alphabetically by location (or postcodes for sat-navs) rather than name, unless your memory for such things is a lot better than mine.

2. Backyard Food

Whether traveling in Mediterranean areas, Eastern Europe, or Southeast Asia, I quickly became aware of how nearly everyone's "backyard" was really productive. There were chickens, rabbit hutches, small but highly productive vegetable beds and/or containers, and fruit trees or bushes trained up walls and fences.

I note the same productivity in the urban gardens of Burmese acquaintances, local Polish contacts, and Irish musician mates, all here in England. In adopting city life, many British folk seem to have lost touch with their agrarian past and food-growing traditions; the state of the world and global food requirements mean that we should challenge that lethargy—wherever.

All of us with some space can grow something, even if it is just tomatoes, herbs, and few salad items, on an apartment balcony or window ledge. I visited some folks in a downtown terrace that had a tiny backyard where there were wall-mounted troughs, with cascades of tomatoes and strawberries, as well as an espaliered plum tree, a raised bed of herbs and lettuce, and a table big enough for six of us to eat a meal at. I have raised beds and cold frames in the front garden and backyard of my corner cottage. Water butts and drainpipe adaptors are often much cheaper to buy in winter sales—so use the free rain.

3. Batterie de cuisine

This is just the cookery books' posh phrase for your kitchen kit. It is worth reviewing what you have got, as well as what you really need on a day-to-day basis. Logically, what you need can change as a family grows or a household contains more lodgers who cook independently. Rather than having to store my apple-press or largest jam and stock pans in my small galley kitchen, local friends keep and use them and I call them back when I actually need them.

I can make out the case for keeping a good food processor or bulk yoghurt maker (assuming your household eats yoghurt, at least seasonally, by the bucketload) but is it worth wasting space on a bread-maker or anything else if it gets less than regular weekly use? Who needs a banana cutter when you have a good set of knives? One of my lifestyle-teaching colleagues runs a "swap shop" for redundant gadgets and surplus pans, etc.

Keep only the kit that works for your household's changing and developing lifestyle—pass on the rest. But equip yourself for your pattern of living. For example, the cooking kit (including pans, crockery, and knives/utensils) for our personal camping holidays are packed ready-to-go on my loft shelves whereas the catering kit for the big group summer camp is boxed-for-travel on the garage shelves.

4. Beans, Peas, Pulses, and Lentils[1]

You don't have to be vegetarian or Asian-in-origin to enjoy including pulses and legumes to expand your household's diet cheaply. Buy them in as large (therefore less expensive) quantities as you can store; then consume but be prepared to wash then soak beans (often overnight), sprout pulses, and simmer lentils into various forms of dhal. Dhals make great fillers and toppings for curries, stews, and brown or basmati rice; serving several dhals together on rice with raita (a minty yoghurt sauce) makes wonderful meals.

Begin by buying canned red kidney or white haricot beans or tinned chick peas and work outwards from there; all are available at virtually every supermarket. I have acquaintances who buy sacks of white haricots then use various of their own home-grown tomatoes and herbs to make enough jars of "baked beans" to see them through the winter.

Garner recipes and start using all manner of beans, (chick) peas, pulses, and lentils, all of which are filling, inexpensive, and aid digestion. *The Sprouters Handbook*[2] is a great reference book in developing the use of these foods. When you've learned what your folks like, ethnic shops will often sell you larger quantities—sometimes by weight but sometimes unlabeled—hence learn to recognize what you want.

1. Elliot, *Bean Book.*
2. Cairney, *Sprouters Handbook.*

5. Bread

Acquaintances with city apartments in Sydney and Chicago both make their own bread regularly. They buy in flour and one has cleverly used a strengthened shelf, above their guest bedroom door, to hold gallon (former ice-cream) containers of different flours to broaden their repertoire. Teaching children to bake gives a skill for life. I have many friends (some are listed in the Acknowledgements—p. ix) who regularly bake all or at least their weekend bread. However, the individual artisan baker, up before dawn to fire the ovens and mix the dough, deserves our custom—simply to ensure that others beyond our guest-lists can taste and enjoy quality bread and not some steam-blown mass-produced loaf.

6. Buffalo

Most buffalo meat is actually from the North American bison—the huge humped creatures of Saturday Western movies and once shot by Buffalo Bill. It is one of the healthiest red meats available and full of flavor. It is now becoming more widely available in England, lowland Scotland, and New Zealand, as much is locally raised, slaughtered, and butchered—a positive "food miles" factor too. Properly frozen, it can hold its flavor for several weeks (unlike quality organic beef which *can* diminish in flavor), so buying from a local producer is easily possible.

In a 100 g/4 oz serving, buffalo has only less than 2.5 g of fat compared with around 10 g for pork and choice beef and nearly 7.5 g for organic chicken, while buffalo is highest in both iron and vitamin B12 content. It should be treated and cooked like select organic beef. I never marinate it but will serve it with either plain buffalo gravy or pepper or cream sauces. Its quality means that if you buy it from the producer, the cost per serving is roughly the same as organic, free-range beef.

7. Buy as Direct as You Can

How locally can you source what you want to buy? Can you buy from butchers who raise their own meat animals? Can you buy from a Community Supported Agriculture or "veggie-box" scheme? Is your milk produced in the county where you live? How many of the profiteering middlemen can you cut out?

8. Chapati (Flour)

Chapati flour is often known as *ata* and is used for all manner of breads on the Indian subcontinent. I have seen it on sale in supermarkets across Britain, Europe, and Australia as well as obviously in so-called Asian shops. It is a finely milled wheat flour that is low in gluten. Chapatis are a great alternative to Western-style breads with many dishes, including Western stews and hearty broths. They can be cooked easily paratha-style (spiced flatbread) on a griddle or in a medium-heat frying pan within minutes; they are a great source of fun when one invites children to be the sous-chefs. Equally, stuffed parathas, with either meat or vegetables, are a meal in themselves and (for me) much more enjoyable than (stuffed) pizza calzone.

9. Charity Shops, Church Sales, and Yard Sales

Just as yard sales are part of the fabric of American suburbs so charity (thrift) shops are part of virtually every UK high street. They are a great source of specialist cookery books, whether food types, particular writers, or regional world styles. If a book looks likes yielding ten-plus good, new recipes, it can be worth three or four dollars to check it out at your leisure *before* returning it to the charity shop of your choice. I also know folks who "cannibalize" such books, razor-blading the relevant pages into their box files of collected recipes then recycling the carnage as waste paper. Obviously the back-to-sale route is more planet Earth-friendly.

These sales are also a great source of kitchen equipment—as is the annual "fair" at your local church. At some shops and fairs, I have sourced non-blown pressure cookers for £1, pristine demijohns for winemaking at a dollar each, large jam pans and stock pots for a couple of quid, as well as sets of copper-bottomed pans, sets of crystal sherry glasses, and a Le Creuset casserole for under a fiver. Thoroughly cleaned, you can easily upgrade your own kit or they can be passed on to friends wanting to expand their *batterie de cuisine* on a budget.

10. Compost

You can compost almost everything organic—but don't worry, compost loos are the subject of some future, as-yet-unplanned book. (There's only one more mention of poo.)

The composting principle is vital now that the feeding of kitchen scraps—even to your own domestic chickens, pig, or goat—is technically illegal (in the UK). Everyone can compost their vegetable/fruit peelings and skins, used tea bags, egg shells, and anything organic that does not have a protein content (as this attracts rats), so never compost bones, meat, or fish leftovers. Those of us blessed with a garden can also add grass-cuttings, plant-trimmings, and other "brown materials" (as twigs, leaves, and woodier vegetation are called). If you have enough compost space, you can compost the used bedding of vegetarian livestock, such as guinea pigs or rabbits, but not cat litter or dog poo.

Those with only small outside spaces can normally house a compost bin, even in a duplex yard—mask it with a climber or runner beans. I stayed in a city high-rise where there was a sophisticated composter kept on their fifth-floor balcony; the resulting compost was used for herbs and balcony boxes. Behind my garage, I have built a frame from scrap lumber used to hold unwanted builders' bags (the large cubic-yard size in which sand and other aggregates are delivered) and created a compost system, which some of my neighbors also use for their garden clippings. One enterprising local allotmenteer offered free, lidded (diaper/nappy-) buckets to all his flat-dwelling neighbors, collecting the contents of their buckets four times a week, which he barrows to his allotment compost heaps. Desire, versatility, and ingenuity could enable far more composting to occur, enriching so much soil.

11. Create a "Collective"

For those of us based in singleton or couple homes rather than shared households, it can be economically, globally, and ecologically important to "band together" to bulk-buy, to share expertise, tools, gluts, and so on. You do not need to be lifelong friends (although that "spin-off" may occur!) but just committed to making your lives significantly more "earth-friendly." You might *all* only meet together a few times per year, but you might run a food cooperative or rent some larger space together for growing. The possibilities are endless.

12. Dining Out

How and where we choose to eat, outside the home, says much about us. In the UK and USA, legislation demands that food set on a diner's table has to be thrown away (i.e., not reused) if it is not consumed—so I try to avoid those restaurants that put dishes of food on my table. It is far better to go to a servery or salad cart or dessert trolley for the extras. Sometimes when preaching in Oxford, I eat with friends in a riverside pub that serves different sizes of adult meals to cater for differently sized appetites and avoid waste—how wise.

13. Eggs—"Free-Range, of course"

The case for free-range eggs has already been made. It is almost the easiest change that *every* household can make. Every supermarket stocks free-range eggs—also often in their "value" or own-brand label, even if it comes in flimsy cardboard (which can be as easily composted or recycled!). I have yet to discover a local veg-box scheme that does not also supply free-range eggs—even if sometimes you have to supply a suitably sized, empty egg box the week before. And if you are blessed enough to keep your own chickens, well done!

14. (So-Called) Ethnic Shops

The UK is a mongrel nation, tracing its roots back through Huguenots and Normans, to Angles, Saxons, Vikings, and Celts. Some shops are so-called "ethnic shops" but are often run by second-, third-, and fourth-generation British shopkeepers, with Afro-Caribbean, Asian, East-European, and both Near- and Far-Eastern roots—all of whom are as British as I am. The same is true in Australian and American conurbations. These shops are a wonderland. Do not be afraid to wait and ask what particular foods, fruit, flours, and spices actually are—then buy and try something; if you ask politely, you will be offered advice on its preparation and cooking.

I have learned much from Asian shopkeepers and my neighbors in almost-ethnic ghettoes as well as, for instance, from the writings of Madhur Jaffrey.[3] Shopping in multiethnic cities taught me so much about Caribbean cuisine. Take a slight detour on city journeys and learn as you shop. Thanks

---

3. Jaffray, *Indian Cookery*.

to north African package holidays, most of us now accept tagines and couscous as part of our weekly lives. A cosmopolitan diet is rich, inexpensive, and often very healthy when things are cooked well.

15. Farm Shops and Farmers' Markets

One rural colleague tells me his wife has altered her rural school run to the other two sides of their possible diamond-shaped route, taking her daily past a farm shop. He says their diet has improved, at no extra cost, as she now buys fresh vegetables in their glut, organic honey, free-range eggs, and sacks of potatoes, carrots, and onions. Most urbanites can regularly find their travels take them past a good farm store; it is then a matter of planning to have the time to stop and buy. The first UK farmers' market was in Bath in 1997 and now virtually every UK town or city has one. They provide an alternative to farm shops for those who are more restricted in their traveling.

16. Fish

In smaller countries or those with good shorelines, fish is a great source of protein. Get hold of some good fish-cookery books[4] that deal with your region. I remember seeing a cyclostyled catfish-recipe book in an Appalachian store. So expand your food tastes—eat more fish, fresh, frozen, or even canned.

17. Flour

Using different kinds of flour is not only healthier but demands learning and versatility in home-baking. Even urbanites (see "Bread" above) can store several flours in restricted living space. In 2014, the UK began statutorily insisting that commercially sold bread flour must have folic acid added to it (similar to US and Canadian legislation) to lessen the incidence of spina bifida in human embryo development. Although you can improve your diet without expanding your living space or your waistline, checking the additives to any raw flour is something to be aware of.

4. E.g., Grigson and Black, *Fish.*

18. Food Cooperatives

Friends set up a food cooperative with about twelve products. They bought flour by the sack, olive oil by the five-gallon drum, and honey in a two-gallon barrel. They bought four popular varieties of beans, two of lentils, and porridge/oatmeal by the sack. They also used to buy chick peas, canned tomatoes, and fish, etc., by the case from their local supermarket, charging US5c/3p more per can. Because everyone brought their own containers to the monthly meeting, there were no public health issues nor legislation problems. I have just helped another group to set up an internet version of this but based across a small town.

Is this something your household or "collective" should be doing?

19. Free Recipes and Food Ideas

Several supermarkets publish free quarterly magazines. Our collective circulates them, copying/cutting out recipes and utilizing much of the cooking/growing information before recycling what's left. We also do the same with our daily newspapers; the "Food and Drink" supplement from my Thursday copy of *The Times* normally passes through at least two more households; those friends reciprocate with their weekend magazine supplements. Between us, we are compiling a library of information covering a breadth of food-related issues, as well as recipes, based on our own interests and family needs. If we are really stuck, we just type in what we need to our internet search engine. Many of the ideas in this book began life around someone's kitchen table after the prompting of such an article or recipe.

20. Freezer

Do not run your freezers all year round. Keep one especially for the autumn glut to help you overwinter your blanched-but-fresh gluts (see below). Most of all, learn the techniques to freeze and defrost the flavor in.[5] Basements or a lockable outhouse are great places for large freezers—then just bring stuff in weekly to your smaller kitchen freezer.

5. Rubinstein and Bush, *Penguin Freezer Cookbook*.

21. Gluts

Try to be prepared for gluts of anything—share them, give them away, bottle or freeze them, make jams or chutneys. This is where both your "collective" and/or food cooperative can help. Local greengrocers often sell off trays of soft fruit at the end of Saturday afternoons (if their shops are closed on Sundays)—I got a whole tray (9 kg) of peaches for 50 pence/US 75c and bottled the lot. One near neighbor with several apple trees puts tubs of their fruit on his garden wall for any passer-by to take. Our local allotment group has a sheltered table where growers place their harvested excess veg, and informal exchange means nothing goes to waste, or even to the compost bins.

One novice allotmenteer returned from holiday to find such a surplus of gone-over runner beans that we helped her and her partner make 17 lb of delicious runner-bean chutney—something else they had never done before. Don't forget that UK readers can easily bring back cheap sacks of onions and garlic from an autumn break in France. I know a couple who bring back sacks of red and white onions from their annual October visit, making wonderful chutneys on their return

22. Grow Your Own

Get hold of some land and start growing your own food, whether in small raised beds or pots. Remember to compost to help refresh the soil *and* rotate the crops. Start with growing something you really enjoy but which is expensive in the shops, even when in season.

We use grow-bags and some extra, bought-in, used, peat-free compost, which, if it has just been growing root or salad crops, can be spread and hoed directly into our raised beds at the end of the season, whereas the root-ridden tomato grow-bags need to go through the compost system. We also overwinter most of our raised beds with deciduous leaf mulch, weighted down with old strawberry netting; the combination of worms and weather suppresses weed-growth, and the leaf-goodness breaks up and goes down into the soil. It is a free and dig-free way of adding compost. This kind of no-dig gardening is a branch of permaculture.

23. Guerrilla Gardeners

This is the practice of secret urban gardeners to plant up unused spaces of earth with a food crop. They try to tend and nurture the crop without identity-detection. I saw a stretch of urban freeway that had its chain-link boundary fence, next to a small housing project, planted with climbing beans, zucchini/courgettes and small squashes. Johnny Appleseed never knew what he was starting.

24. Hedgerow Food[6]

In my everyday shoulder bag that goes virtually everywhere with me, I always carry the pocket-size *Food for Free*[7] (as well as a portable chess set and a New Testament) and a couple of food-bags. Wherever, I am, I can check on the identification of seasonal berries, edible mushrooms, and other hedgerow foods. On common land they are free to the picker and, used quickly, are delicious. Both the book and food-bags are of little use if left on my hallway shelf if the opportunity for "wild-foraged" or hedgerow food presents itself.

I chose to live within 100 yards of an urban woodland pathway; many of my local friends live along its route. Throughout the year, we pick the gluts of nuts, berries, mushrooms, nettles, and elderflowers—for straight consumption, incorporation into salads, or making jams and country wines. As I visit friends or speak at conferences across the country, I encourage others to recognize that such "forage" as hedgerow food provides is nutritious and available; but never take everything—allow some for others and next season's growth for another harvest.

Across the UK:

- Lancashire friends have discovered that the former railway lines, now cycle-ways, between Pennine mill towns are great forage grounds.

- Norfolk acquaintances have taught me when to visit so I can check the tidal samphire beds.

- East Midlands colleagues call when Sherwood's mushrooms arrive.

These latter are occasional treats occurring when business takes me in their direction in the due season; otherwise I become part of the "food miles" stupidity. Have you found such local "hedgerows" yet?

6. Wright, *Hedgerow.*
7. Mabey, *Food for Free.*

It behoves those of us who live on or near the coast to find an expert who can guide us to the *safe* pickings from the shoreline.[8]

These examples demonstrate that food foraging is a nationwide opportunity.[9] In the Americas and Australasia, such foraging presents even greater possibilities

25. Herbs

All herbs are best used when fresh. One way to keep them is to chop them finely, put meal-size portions in ice-cube trays, cover with water, and freeze them; then just use the appropriate herb cube(s) straight from the freezer in any recipe. Two contact Oxbridge families spend their summers at their respective Scottish and French homes; both take living pots of their commonly used herbs, keeping them on a windowsill and cutting them freshly as necessary.

Those of us with a single base of operation and enough space could grow a herb wheel, beloved of permaculturists,[10] where a two- or three-yard wide rising spiral of earth is planted serially with different herbs, those requiring more shade on its north side. If space precludes this, one former colleague grew herbs in plastic buckets on his sixth-floor balcony. I adapted this, using a rhino tub for each herb, predrilling their bases for drainage, but it allows me to move herbs into shade or sunlight according to their needs; most are within five metres of my kitchen door, enabling their rapid harvesting when needed.

26. Honey

Drinks in a Bronx backyard and a grill on a London roof-terrace both had me standing too close to my respective host's beehives; both their honeys had delicious and distinctive tastes. Wiltshire neighbors and rural friends all produce their own honeys. A 1 lb/450 g jar attractively presented is a great small gift or more plainly as a currency for barter. Try replacing honey for sugar in some of your dessert recipes, using it on your breakfast oatmeal or a spoonful as you make curries . . . then ask why you don't join a

8. Wright, *Edible Seashore.*

9. Those in the USA, Canada, Australasia, and continental Europe need to apply this variety to their own geographical and climactic context.

10. Mollison, *Introduction to Permaculture*, 96.

beekeeping group. Some give you so many pounds of honey for each hive you can accommodate.

27. "Incredible, Edible Todmorden"[11]

In Todmorden, Yorkshire, in the north of England, what began as guerrilla gardening has become a pattern of local life. Across the town, packed with small, terraced homes, spare or empty spaces are being converted into growing spaces as community allotments. Verges are being planted with fruit bushes. Planters in areas like the high street or bus and train stations are being used for vegetable growing. Local primary schools and newspaper columns are all teaching that local food production is the right way to go—and for everyone who is fit and able to share in it. More shops are stocking seeds, wellie boots, and adverts for tools, redundant sheds, etc.

Whether or not it is Todmorden's example, many other similar local initiatives are occurring nationwide across England. In Birmingham, a small brownfield site has become a community allotment, guaranteed for the next few years, thanks to local councilor support. Recently, a builder in Bristol offered a private site, a secure shed, and some literal seed-money to a neighborhood group as a community veg plot while he awaited planning permission to develop this and an adjoining parcel of land, a couple of years later. In a Norfolk village, the parish council liberated some bequeathed scrubby pasture to become more allotments for locals. A Londoner, whose family had a Devon holiday home, leased the accompanying field to the parish council at £10 per annum, "providing it is used as allotments for local people."

Just as with the Hugh Fearnley-Whittingstall Landshare Scheme,[12] there is a growing creativity—if you will pardon the pun—in the way we can use these crowded islands.

Not all of us can live in Todmorden, but theirs and these other examples can become the inspiration for many other local initiatives. Even if you do not have land or even a garden, you may live close to a site that could be so utilized even if only for a few years. What each opportunity

11. This phrase has been used by Todmorden residents as well as their local media but was popularized in August 2010 by the BBC's Colette Hume as she accompanied the Prince of Wales on his "green tour" of the UK to both promote and celebrate "whole earth thinking" and eco-responsibility.

12. www.landshare.com

needs is someone to spot the potential and then gather a few others (a good excuse for a shared meal) to plan towards making it happen.

28. Jars and Bottles

Never recycle a glass jar or bottle that has a screw-top lid—at least, not until you have considered its potential for reuse. Shop-bought ketchup can yield glass bottles (with screw lids), which are perfect for storing home-produced yellow, green, and red tomato ketchups as well as other vegetable (e.g., beetroot or garlic or mushroom or onion, etc.) sauces.

Small olive oil bottles can be well recycled as presents containing home-produced fruit vinegars, ketchups, and sauces, as well as oil with home-produced herbs or garlic infusing them.

Obviously, all jam and marmalade jars can be reused, as can most mayonnaise, chutney, and (except the most pungent) pickle jars. Even those tiny jars you get on ferries or with cream teas are great for sending herbs or spices with school children or to your evening class or for a family's weekend camping.

So always wash both the glass and the lids properly and store while checking with your collective. Remember to store any pickle or vinegar-based product jars separately from the rest as the lids will be tainted. So who in your collective makes jams, chutneys, ketchups, pickles, and specialist oils to pass them on to? Some of our other friends provide us with clean jars/bottles and lids; they know that for every ten empty jars or so, they will get one returned full of a jam or chutney or ketchup of their choice.

29. Knives and Utensils

Although I will buy named (e.g., Sabatier, the Cook's Company, etc.) kitchen knives from charity shops and the like, I buy new wooden and other utensils only from reputable kitchen shops. The exception to that can be local authority sales of surplus school institutional stock, which is often stainless steel or sufficiently heavy duty to be properly sterilized before use. We used such a sale to purchase enough mass-catering kit for our group's annual summer camp.

30. Labeling[13]

This book has explained why we need accurate labeling that includes the weight and exact nature of the content's ingredients, as well as what the product is, e.g., baked beans. But what more do we want? Deceptive pictures of rural idyllic production and excess promotional guff tell you more about the producers' motives than the product you are buying. The simplest protest is to choose a better-labeled version of that product; if it is your favorite thing, write to the manufacturer, enclosing the offending label or packet—and remember to ask for a personal reply. Check out what your government produces.[14]

31. Learn the Origins of the Food You Buy

"Learn the origins of the food that you buy and buy food that is produced closest to your home. The idea that every locality should be, as much as possible, the source of its own food makes several kinds of sense. The locally produced food supply is the most secure, the freshest, and the easiest for local consumers to know about and influence."[15]

32. Leftover Wine and Cooking Sherry

Friends laughed when they read the draft of this paragraph, shouting, "What do you mean—leftover wine?" I was never a fan of screw-top wine bottles but they have become a boon for cooks. Don't squeeze that last inch out of the bottle at supper or the end of the evening; decant it to your cooking bottles. Keep one white and one red. But do use it, quickly—no one wants extra vinegar added to piquant recipes. Remember that if used properly, the alcohol content is "burned off" in the cooking process, and it is its flavor that you want. More easily, keep a bottle of fortified English wine (they can't call it sherry) next to the stove and use this in cooking—our local supermarket stocks a brand for about £3/US $5 per bottle.

---

13. Lawrence, *Not On the Label.*

14. E.g., UK Food Standards Agency, *Food Labels—More Informed Choices.*

15. Berry, *Bringing It to the Table,* 232.

33. Markets

In many urban environments, there is a designated weekly market, sometimes daily, where fresh fruit, vegetables, fish, and local cheese and eggs are sold—often alongside many other things, including tools and seeds. In France, half of all families buy all their fruit and vegetables from such markets. Elsewhere, specialist food markets trade every day, such as the fish markets in Venice's Rialto, Corfu town, or northern Portugal, or Monterey's fish-sheds and those on the Florida Keys. The smaller meat markets in the Camargue (France), the Plaka in Athens, or some Canadian cities also serve their purpose well.

34. Marmalade versus Marrow Jam[16]

There will come a point in the future when either the "food miles" question will become so overwhelming or the political situation becomes sufficiently difficult that UK plc will not be able to import the requisite amount of oranges and/or other citrus fruits. The former option is the more likely. All the orangeries in Britain could not produce the amount of fruit required. Californians, the southern French, and Queenslanders can just smile and think how railroading citrus will keep their economies going.

Two key products will be affected in the UK and those states furthest from California's or Queensland's oranges. Orange juice may still be produced from imported concentrate, making this a high-cost luxury product rather than the "value option" such processing deems it to be now. Freshly squeezed orange juice may become a choice of only the super-rich.

Another everyday product that will be affected is marmalade. Last year, we made sufficient marrow jam to convince both ourselves and friends that this was a viable alternative to marmalade. If one decent-size marrow can produce five or six jars of jam, then one square yard for growing four or five such marrows could produce enough "alternative marmalade" for most families.

Without sounding like "prophets of doom," how much do we ever think about the locally sourced alternatives (and have begun using them!) in case Britain, or wherever, for whatever reason, cannot import our former product of choice? In every continent where these books are read, this

16. Marmalade is an archetypal British "jam" used at breakfast with toast; usually its fruit are oranges, but lime or lemon varieties are also available.

principle is the same; some foodstuffs will need locally grown alternative ingredients to replace the currently imported one.

35. Meat

Plan how often your household wants and needs to eat meat. Cultivate a good relationship with a butcher—even the one at the butchery counter of a large supermarket's meat stall, if this is your only option. Discover your local organic meat suppliers. If yours is one of those families who enjoy taking self-catering breaks, with time to cook on a campfire or cabin stove, don't be afraid to ask at the local butcher's if something in his window looks unfamiliar when you are away from home.

It is nutritionally better to buy a cheaper cut of organic meat than a supposedly better cut from an unknown source at the supermarket. So buy a shoulder of pork rather than loin for roasting or buy pork cheek rather than pork steaks for grilling. You can apply the same principles to beef or lamb, in Britain, *cheval* in Europe, and goat in Asia. If you buy organic chicken thighs, take the skin off to reduce the fat intake. They are just as good as any breast meat but they can be cheaper than nonorganic chicken breast.

36. Older Can Be Wiser!

After I recounted our marrow-jam episode at an international conference, someone sent me a photocopy of their East Anglian (UK) grandmother's wartime recipe, which also suggested this alternative, using surplus honeycomb and home-pulped sugar beet to provide the sugar, while an Adelaide visitor sent me a photocopy of the typewritten wartime recipe book, produced by their neighborhood church. While I am not advocating going back to powdered egg, Camp coffee, and other "nasties" (as remembered by my parents!), wartime recipe books can help us devise many different homegrown alternatives to imported foodstuffs.

37. One Is Fun!

The number of single people in the Westernized nations is growing, whether through choice, divorce, or bereavement, and that number is projected to grow. Look how many supermarkets stock a "meals for one" range. Also increasing numbers of couples have to live apart during their working weeks, effectively creating more single person households. Often this will mean smaller living spaces, less storage, and cramped kitchen facilities. However, some of the most creative and earth-friendly cooks I know are "singletons"—often with such limited space. In the UK, books by TV chef Delia Smith[17] and former journalist Katherine Whitehorn[18] illustrate that this is a recognized consumer market.

I know from my own single days that the clue to good (solo-)cooking is to keep a good store cupboard of basics (e.g., canned tomatoes, tinned anchovies, eggs, dried chorizo, herbs and spices, long-life cream, cooking pastes, and olive oil) as well as a small freezer space for stock, fresh but frozen veg, and quality ice-cream. No good butcher or fishmonger will baulk or joke about preparing a cut for a single portion. But it is often the versatility of such singletons in producing an intimate lunch or supper party for three or four folk—sometimes on only a two-ring stove with a steamer—that can inspire the rest of us.

UK professor Roy Strong explained that, following the death of his wife some years ago, he still makes meals an occasion, using table linen and preset cutlery to ensure that eating is not just a matter of refueling. I have another single, divorced colleague who does the same but always lights a candle as well, putting both the answering machine and a favorite CD on, thus ensuring every meal becomes even more pleasurable. Eating alone can be time both to savor flavor and to celebrate the life one has.

38. Packaging

We need to revisit the points on packaging made earlier in this book. Without being offensive to checkout staff or their store's managers, none of us—including the planet—needs anything to be packaged more than is necessary. The point needs to be made repeatedly, so that shops and their suppliers come to a sensible rethink about every product. If we can sell sugar or flour, beans or lentils, coffee beans or own-brand cereals in "single-skin" packets, why can't freeze-dried instant coffee and teabags be sold similarly? Do they need a new jar or a cardboard box around the foil envelope? Just extend the principle . . . and lobby your local shopkeeper or supermarket manager.

17. Smith, *One Is Fun!*
18. Whitehorn, *Cooking in a Bedsitter.*

39. Picky Eaters

Every Westerner has their likes and dislikes—we live without the imperative of real poverty or possible starvation to have to face being forced to eat
anything available. Some of us have genuine medical or allergic conditions,
such as diabetes, celiac conditions, or nut allergies, which involve thinking
about everything we eat. Clearly, human dignity demands that we should
respect the religious traditions or vegetarian principles of those for whom
excluding some items is vital too. But nearly all of us know, have experienced, or still have someone in our household or family who is a picky or
fussy eater.

Such folks tend to baulk generally at one of two things. One is texture.
I can understand how fish, some veg like courgettes or tomatoes, or even
pasta can seem squishy. The cooks for household meals need to work out
longer-term strategies for bringing the tastes to the fore *before textures*,
choosing meatier kinds of fish or baking precooked pasta (as in the Maltese
dishes of timpana or imqarron).

The second is smell and this is more problematic. The reputable Duke
University in North Carolina have just begun a several-year, nationwide,
multi-thousand participant research project that may ultimately show that
"food rejection because of smell" is actually hard-wired in our DNA. Woe
betide us if our children and grandchildren discover this yet-to-be confirmed theory and start saying that genes mean they cannot eat whatever
they dislike the smell of!

However, while we are all entitled to our personal tastes and foibles, it
is vital if we are serious about a "whole earth" diet that we educate our palates to be as wide-ranging as our faith and personal principles allow—even
if that means changing some cooking techniques.

40. Plan Meals with Others

Even atheists advocate eating together, recognizing the "community building" meals of various faith groups—the Hebrew Passover, the Buddhist tea
ceremonies, the Christian Eucharist, even Christmas and Thanksgiving
traditions, while advocating their own monastic-style public refectories.[19]
Whether it is with friends or neighbors, your local book group or "food
collective," or your Christian housegroup/"cell," plan to meet and eat. How
and what you serve graciously helps to get your "earth-friendly" message

19. De Botton, *Religion for Atheists*.

across. Remember two of the French rules of home cuisine: "food is social" and should be shared together; and you do not have to like it, but you ought at least to try it.

41. Polytunnels

These are a practical and portable alternative to a large greenhouse. Smaller versions are now available for the "domestic market." They are great for bringing on early vegetables, maximizing both multi- and tomato-cropping, creating an autumn-into-winter growing season—all obviously protecting what is in them from the excesses of the northern hemisphere weather by creating their own micro-climate. Most gardening allotment magazines carry adverts for inexpensive polytunnels with dimensions to fit many sizes of garden. The opportunity and possibility of using polytunnels to help assist local veg growing, by also extending the season and sheltering seeds, just demands relatively small sites and wise creativity.

42. Pop-Up Restaurants

The term "pop-up restaurants" is applied both to situations when a well-known chef takes over a landmark building and runs a restaurant for a short season within it and to occasions when amateur chefs use a venue, even their own home, as a one-night-stand restaurant venue. The latter are more exciting, discovered by word of mouth, from "alternative" magazines, or a local advert; often you book via mobile phone, then are texted the venue on the day itself and pay by cash only.

Such restaurants can helpfully challenge both our food thinking and our entertaining ideas and ideals. One sophisticated couple served great vegetarian Asian fusion food to cross-legged diners on the floor of newly carpeted but vacant offices—their low tables were linen-covered shuttering boards mounted on bricks. An Anglo-Brazilian couple offered South American food with only a postcard advert, headed "Never eaten alligator?" in a delicatessen; they did admit to using crocodile as they could not locally source alligator! One Polish couple use their small flat (moving their TV and settee into the bedroom), doing various wonders with potatoes, cabbage, gherkins, and cheaper cuts of meat; their digestif of a potato "vodka" meant we all needed taxis home. The occupants of a very English suburban semi-detached house hosted a game roast in its garden, with barbecued boar, venison steaks, all with English berry sauces and real ale; to the neighbors it looked like almost any other grill party.

The variety is incredible, good fun, and a growing trend. One group of Manchester acquaintances do this every term, with no public adverts, when the host family provide both food and the venue but the cash raised goes to the hosts' favorite charity. The possibilities are endless.

43. Porridge/Oatmeal

For centuries, some kind of cereal porridge was a staple part of the diet of the rural poor of Britain. Grain boiled up with a handful of hedgerow "forage" sometimes formed the only meal of the day for the poverty-stricken. Today over 50 percent of rural Africa still survives on mealie porridge.

Porridge is a great breakfast cereal and easily personalized. Try soaking the oats overnight in a covered pan on the central-heating boiler or woodstove. East Anglian treacles, home-produced honey, garden fruit compotes or hedgerow nuts or any combination can turn a goodly portion into a meal. Non-drivers may even add a wee dram to the "overnight soak" to give a Scotch flavor. An acquaintance runs a boarding house for working Polish émigrés, daily serving differently flavored porridge by the gallon before they are picked up for construction work.

Porridge is nutritious, inexpensive, and can use locally produced oats (check the packaging!), meeting the needs of both families and the manual worker. A little planning means one can work from oats and first principles, not the prepackaged alternatives, which often include a raft of additives. Campaign for real porridge!

44. "Prepare Your Own Food"

"This means reviving in your own mind and life the arts of kitchen and household. This should enable you to eat more cheaply, and it will give you a measure of 'quality control.' You will have some reliable knowledge of what has been added to the food you eat."[20]

20. Berry, *Bringing It to the Table*, 232.

45. Pressure Cookers

These are the steamers of my mom's generation, enabling several things to be cooked separately at the same time, or much more quickly, such as steamed puddings. There is an art to cooking with them and beware the scalding steam from the valve, which must be released before taking off the lid. If you buy one secondhand, check it still has its inner "baskets," its pressure valve, and a flat bottom. After twenty years of use, I gave mine away and now use a steamer—see below.

46. Rabbit

Until the 1950s, rabbit was the most popular everyday UK meat. Most rabbit was shot rather than commercially farmed and sold by virtually every local butcher and fishmonger. Rabbit in the postwar British diet had the same ubiquity and popularity as chicken does today. It was the ravages of myxomatosis that ended rabbit's popularity then. This trend needs reversing. As a meat, rabbit is so versatile, lending itself to roasting, stewing, pies, barbecuing, or spicing up as curry, "Tex-Mex," etc.

Unless wild-shot, rabbit is really suited to small-scale production. I know some families in Birmingham, England, who hardly ever eat any meat except rabbit, which they breed in their own backyards. In France, one of my village neighbors bred rabbit both for the pot and to barter for a couple of jars of home-made preserves, a bowl of fruit (my Morello cherry tree proved popular) or a bottle of someone's garden vintage. All your rabbits need, once they are housed securely, is a basic rabbit-pellet diet, which can be well-supplemented with potato-peel mash, vegetable tops from the allotment, and the odd seedy lettuce, again emphasizing rabbits' potential as a backyard meat. Even rabbit pelts can be home-cured—this needs only a small scraping frame, salt, and time—to make delightfully warm blankets.

These examples point towards how rabbit could become part of a new barter economy along with backyard free-range eggs, line-caught fish, and surplus allotment vegetables. Like organic chicken and buffalo, rabbit is one of the healthiest meats in terms of good protein and low fat content.

47. Seasonal Food

Do you really need to have strawberries in January? Or honeydew melon as the light starter before Christmas dinner? Some foods are best enjoyed when they are seasonal and a variety of different tastes and textures appear throughout the year.

One country acquaintance makes bottles of strawberry coulis when the fruit is in glut, serving that coulis with home-made plain yoghurt on spongecake as a winter dessert. Seasonal creativity is the key to changing our eating habits.

Throughout the year, one Salisbury couple's former (now white-washed) coal bunker has been converted into a food store by their adult son and his girlfriend, whose monthly visits often involve gathering local fruit or buying seasonal gluts at market, to make jams, chutneys, and country wines at that parental home, before taking each month's supply back to their designer London-Barbican flat.

There are also global and economic decisions spurring on the increase of people purchasing more local and seasonal food. In the UK, the "Eat Seasonably Campaign" patiently encourage the understanding that to eat foods in their season creates a healthier diet, and fosters variety and tastier food, all in a better way for our planet.

48. Seeds and Spices and Nuts

Apply the lessons from "Beans, Peas, Pulses, and Lentils" (above) to seeds, spices, and nuts. Vegetarian curries or stews with seeds and/or nuts as the protein are delicious and "Earth-friendly."

49. Share-Cropping or Community Supported Agriculture Schemes

As CSA schemes become more popular globally, they often give long-term discounts to founding, and sometimes funding members. To share the ownership of some productive land "collectively" is a model for change and for the future.

50. Soups

Home-made soups are nutritious and delicious—well worth the time and effort to perfect your favorite recipes, for solo, family, and group eating. If you can't begin with a good home-produced stock (see below), because of storage space, always buy good-quality stock cubes. A hearty vegetable soup, made with any leftover veg, and some freshly baked bread can be a meal on a winter's day; my household often choose to grate some parmesan on top. Even a vegetable soup can enlivened with some chopped prosciutto or leftover meat (try freezing small bags of chopped ends of cold, roasted joints for just this purpose) to pander to those who claim they need animal protein; you can add this bowl by bowl.

Time defeats us all. But inexpensive cans of soup can also be enlivened. Try adding a herb and some wine to the canned soup *before* cooking it gently. For example,

- Basil and a dash of red to tomato;
- Ginger and a little white to chicken;
- Mixed herbs and white to mushroom; or
- Coarse-ground black pepper and cooking sherry to oxtail.

This "cheat" gives you great-tasting home-produced flavors. If some soup manufacturer comes up with "Make every can a gourmet meal" with these ideas, I would like the royalties—please.

51. Start Small

Commit yourself to making changes. At conferences, I advocate that you add another change each university/school semester/term to your shopping policy. Buying free-range eggs or fair-traded coffee/tea is a simple beginning. Then just let it increase from there. Another alternative is to use an additional recycling practice as one of those regular changes. I equally advocate that my conference listeners attempt to grow something each year; some with gardens, yards, or land can add something new incrementally each year. Just as that US correspondent now grows herbs in the sixth-floor windows of his New York brownstone so some Sheffield (in northern England) acquaintances grow tomatoes in pots on their apartment's balcony. Several folks have adopted our pattern of growing herbs in separate flexible polytubs (see above), moving them into sun, shade, or rainfall as necessary.

52. Steamers

Invest in a steamer—preferably one for the cooker/Aga rather than a plug-in electric one. These metal cooking pots enable you to cook normally three different levels of food all on one burner or ring. Some Asian steamers are made from bamboo but still require cooking over a pan of boiling water—and they are more difficult to wash up afterwards. You can improvise using a lidded metal colander over a pan cooking something else. Steamers are energy-efficient and ideal for cooking in small spaces or "on the road." Most good supermarkets sell steamers for less than £15/US $25. It says much for the cause of steamers that they are hardly ever seen in charity shops or yard sales.

53. Tomatoes

Assuming you are a nonsmoker, tomatoes are among the easiest high-quality veg to grow. Nicotined fingers damage tomato plants as tobacco and tomatoes are part of the same plant genus. For the rest of us, they are great food; eaten fresh from the vine, they taste superb. We grow red beef, salad, and cherry tomatoes as well as yellow, black, and tiger-stripe varieties—mainly in grow-bags and pots, against walls, fences, or cane-frame support—all close to the kitchen door. I have picked, washed, chopped, and served to the table a multicolored tomato salad in under three minutes to the joy and amusement of drop-in guests.

Any surplus can be made into chutneys or ketchup. To make and offer both yellow and green tomato chutneys is easy for any serious to-mato-grower. It takes only a couple of seasons to become one of those, as tomatoes are one of the simplest crops to grow for novice gardeners, thus building confidence. As said above, it only takes a difference in recipe and a little confidence to encourage you to make your own red, green, and yellow tomato ketchups; they store easily, retaining their flavor when well-made. Some Herefordshire friends purloined large mayo and jam jars from their local café, so they now are able to bottle enough home-grown tomatoes (prick and drop in boiling water to peel the skins off) that they never buy canned tomatoes; an open jar lasts them up to three days in the fridge.

54. Urban Harvesting

Drive through the outskirts of Australian cities, North American suburbs, or English towns and you will see unpicked but ripe fruit trees. In 2009 in London, a really good urban harvesting scheme began.[21] This is gradually compiling a list of locations and a roster of volunteers. Using the internet,

21. www.abundancelondon.com

they put together convenient sessions for pickers to converge *with permission* to pick the fruit together. The fruit is sorted, and the best is sold to local restaurants and cafés, with the profits used to fund community events, while the more damaged fruit is given to the pickers who promise to use it for jams, pickles, etc.

55. Use "Leftovers"[22]

Remember there is no such thing as leftovers. A French *aubergiste* (country innkeeper) scrapes every serving plate's bones and veg into a large vat on his kitchen's woodstove, boiling it all up gently for tomorrow's stock. Meat and fish bones, in my view, should be simmered up into concentrate then date-stored and frozen in square tubs, which stack more easily, for later use. Leftover veg can be liquidized into soup. Stale bread can be toasted into savory rusks or ground into crumbs for use as a stew or casserole topping. Overripe fruit can be destined and made into *rumtopf* or fruit coulis while browning bananas make a great addition into pancakes or into a sweet-dough for banana-bread. Washed vegetable peelings can be liquidized into smoothies or soup-base; dirty peelings go to the compost or chicken-mash.

56. "Yasu, Kyrie"

I had returned for another doctoral summer school at Princeton. On my first morning back, I bumped into a professor and we went into the refectory to breakfast together. I greeted the Hispanic cook by name and in Spanish. "Hey, Mr. Small Portions, you're back" was his reply in English as he rushed to pump my hand. The professor shook his head, explaining, "Normally, we do not make these connections."

I have always made a point of getting to know the domestic staff, the cooks, the gardeners, and security team wherever I'm staying; as so often they are part of an ignored ethnic group. At Princeton, they got to know I did not want to eat US-size portions—I take just enough and clear my plate. No waste!

Whether I am seeking food on a Greek island or in a North African souk, to know enough Greek or Arabic to politely greet my potential hosts pays every dividend, including often their generosity. The same courtesy is

---

22. Colqhoun, *Thrifty Cookbook.*

true with store owners in the American Midwest, rural France, the Spanish hill-towns, or down-under in Australia.

57. Yoghurt

If your household eats yoghurt daily, consider making your own. Just one serious comparison of the labels on the back of your favorite branded yoghurts will show you how much calorie, sugar, and fat content they have. Of course, every yoghurt will have a fat content because it is a dairy product, as fruit yoghurts will have sugar content because of natural fructose.

I know commuters, city-flat residents, suburban families, and country dwellers who all make their own yoghurt. Most use a bought yoghurt-maker, although some ingeniously use large vacuum flasks. The key is to start with a good yoghurt culture—that "live" yoghurt that acts as the activator for the milk (we use skimmed milk). It is also important to start with a new culture every few weeks. But as one pot of sufficient "live" yoghurt costs less than a quality fruit or split-pot yoghurt, you save money every time you make some more for your folks' use.

US readers who live below the poverty line can apply for government-provided, silver-canned "Commodities" that include milk powder that really works well for yoghurt-making.

13

Developing a Global Strategy

SOME YEARS AGO, THERE was a popular African song on the circuits of community workers and radical Christians called "Harambee." This repetitive work-chant from Kenya means "Let's pull together" in Swahili. It signifies that a community cannot make progress unless there is a corporate effort to change things in a new or particular direction.

For a couple of years (until work took me across the country), I was part of a team that had a weekly market stall under a banner stating Harambee. We sold Traidcraft goods, wholefoods, local pottery and crafts, incense, and radical booklets. We always made enough profit to pay for our pitch, petrol, publicity, and other expenses. We believed we could change the world and had lots of supporters and weekly customers.

Any form of societal change is slow and only gradually incremental unless caused by revolution or natural disaster, such as famine or climate change. Personal change can happen very quickly providing we can reinforce our new-found values with the support of others. So to answer, "What in God's name are you eating?" may require not just a change of diet but a change of values. The latter will have to become acceptable to your household and kinship group quickly, which can be much easier if you work as a small group who share those values with the same common purpose of creating change.

Working Together

The Harambee stall arose when a group of friends, who ran an informal food cooperative together, talked over a meal about doing something more. Although the stall disappeared when the local market closed, the food cooperative has grown and now operates out of a small independent church, delivering folks' internet orders on a Thursday evening.

Churches and neighborhood community groups are full of expertise in working together. In these times of social fragmentation and/or human isolation, they can be the replacement for personal kinship groups. Nothing binds a group together better than eating together or a project with a common purpose. Combining planning or specific preparation for a project over a meal obviously and effectively does both. The use of frequent potluck meals in North American Protestant and Mennonite churches bears testimony to that.

In classic social theory, Sprott delineated a group's travel down a helix with four recurring and successive phases of "forming—storming—norming—performing."[1] This recognizes that groups have to cohere, pushing themselves backwards and forwards in order to establish their groundrules, before they can function effectively.

At a neighborhood level, we have to be patient if we gather a group of folks together to address questions of diet, shopping, and food production. We have to let questions arise and individual voices be heard, to enable creative attitudes to evolve. But it will take a visionary person to catch the idea and gather such a group to address these issues. Are you that person?

In Britain, a charity called the Trussell Trust has established food banks in nearly ninety towns. Each food bank relies on a local group of volunteers to give lists of needs to shoppers, who then just buy a couple of those items and put them in the waiting food bank carts as they exit. Those collected goods are then distributed as food parcels to families and individuals in financial crisis without food. In France, the *Croix Rouge* (Red Cross) undertakes similar supermarket collections, using local groups of supporters, to collect goods for international aid charities. These two examples, and that of the Harambee stall, demonstrate that a small committed group of local volunteer-supporters can make a difference for those less fortunate, while ensuring their donors or customers naturally encounter the questions and issues involved.

1. Sprott, *Human Groups*.

Some Strategic Thinking

Strategic thinking works at two levels—the personal and the corporate. Both levels also need applying at local and global levels. "Think global—act local." Our personal agendas can never be divorced from the corporate and global agendas.

Peter Meadows, the Director of Church Action for World Vision UK, demonstrated a 2003 shopping list contrasting different needs:[2]

What it would cost to:

- Help the world feed itself   £5.5 billion or US $8 billion

- Provide the world with clean water £6 billion or US $9 billion

- Provide universal primary education £4 billion or US $6 billion

What the world already spends:

- On the military   £520 billion or US $780 billion

- On illegal drugs   £267 billion or US $400 billion

- On perfumes   £8 billion or US $12 billion

This is all a question of priorities. Globally these inequalities seem mad, yet how many individuals are working to change them? In February 2013, I heard a CNN report claiming that the cost to the USA of maintaining military air cover for their present Middle East operations is approximately $15 billion per year. When the USA withdraws from Afghanistan and Iraq totally, will enough Americans have federally lobbied the USA (the land of the brave and the home of the free) that their nation alone will have funded sufficient projects to enable the world to feed itself? The answer to that is in the hands of individuals' thought, commitment, and action.

Not all of us are good at strategic thinking nor seeing the "big picture." This is another reason why working as part of a small neighborhood, or even internet, collective can be beneficial. I am part of an online reading group and once per month, we hold an ongoing conversation about that month's book; what began as a theological resource now encompasses economics, ecology, and social justice. But I am also part of a neighborhood collective that meets regularly for meals, serious conversation, and planning government lobbying strategy while passing around our latest challenging books. But, do note, this latter group eats together; long ago

2. Meadows, *Rich Thinking*, 133.

we abandoned the "who does the best supper party" mentality (I doubt we ever had it!) in favor of "whole earth" food, shared-preparation, and often planned pot-lucks. The way we learn together can speak of our strategy in everyday conversation, just as much as in direct answer to the neighbor who wants to know what we are doing.

Adopt a "Whole Earth" Diet

So what is this "whole earth" diet? It is the present-day equivalent of the Charles Elliott's Chinese peasant diet. It is a globally responsible diet. As mentioned in chapter 9, "L-O-AF" should mean adopting local, organic, and animal-friendly as first principles.

But then we have to recognize that we cannot grow coffee or tea in Michigan or bananas in my British backyard or oranges in Tasmania. We then have to commit ourselves to Fairtrade/Transfair purchasing. Yes, and this will mean paying more for all these daily commodities than we do now. It will mean paying more for local flour to make *more* of our own bread and pasta. But if we buy better quality *and* less quantity of locally sourced meat, we *should* also save money. Equally, if we *can* join a local community gardening group to grow vegetables, we will get fresher and much less expensive produce for our tables. We can drink more iced tap-water and use hedgerow cordials for cold-in-the-summer and hot-in-the-winter drinks. Our personal food budget does not have to increase—indeed many vegetarians will argue that it can significantly decrease. Chapter 12, "Start Here," begins to provide that compendium of ideas.

We have to re-educate our Westernized minds and palates towards a different kind of diet. We need to eat more seasonally, using the available vegetables, fish, or meat, learning to bottle or freeze our surpluses for future days. We probably should drink less tea and coffee; this may help as we seek to reduce our sugar intake. We need to cut out processed foods, sugary-cereals, over-packaged goodies, TV dinners or "ready meals" from our regular eating. We need to reduce our "fast food," takeaway, and diner-on-the-run patterns. Two of Britain's most popular family meals are vegetarian—beans-on-toast and egg-and-chips/fries—we should eat more vegetarian meals. We should prepare more of our meals from single, known ingredients, whether fresh, frozen, bottled, or canned. We need to want to make such changes—and working with a group or large shared household makes that easier.

145

Our neighborhood collective often buys secondhand cookery books, then we lend them to each other; we make dated notes and comments in the margins. If a particular title proves to be really useful in moving towards a "whole earth" diet several of us may end up acquiring our own household's copies. The various "Moosewood" titles[3] and the Mennonite *More-with-Less Cookbook*[4] and *Extending the Table*[5] volumes seem to be recurring favorites, with their recipes well-tried on many appreciative folks. Trying new foods or recipes and sharing expertise is a way of learning, appreciating, and developing a "whole earth" diet.

If you are a confident cook, you could begin a pop-up restaurant serving whole earth food.[6]

What Can Your Church Do?

Some years ago, I regularly preached within a small radically oriented congregation who met in a large carpeted room above a midtown high-street store. They had another large room with tables and a kitchen area, where they held twice-weekly "whole-earth" meals. They ran a weekly stall, similar to the previously described Harambee stall, were prayerfully committed to various social justice initiatives, and many lived in shared households. But they had their shared library of cookbooks, campaign leaflets, radical theology books, and "community-builders" on shelves in that dining room. It had taken them twenty years to get this far—so be patient and take small steps to continue your journey.

Churches or even their small "cells" and house-groups can be a tremendous force for social change. "Congregations committed to ministering to people in need sometimes overlook their greatest resource—the fellowship of believers."[7] Whether it was our Harambee group or the three couples who began a church using safari suppers, a small group of Christians committed to a specific common cause can help change the mindset of a congregation's majority. In turn, they all have friends, neighbors, and workplace colleagues whom they can influence. One of my pre-publication readers, with her pastor's agreement, handed out "What in God's name are

3. Put "Moosewood cookery books" in your search engine and await the avalanche.
4. Longacre, *More-with-Less Cookbook*.
5. Schlabach, *Extending the Table*.
6. *Sunday Times*, Home section, December 11, 2011.
7. Pohl, *Making Room*, 159.

you eating?" leaflets, inviting folks to a series of three evening meals, to discuss the issues that you have read about in the preceding pages; she is now recruiting her second group. Individuals can make real differences.

In all my past congregations, I have found a couple of motivated individuals who have run Fairtrade stalls. All those churches moved to becoming Fairtrade churches—serving only fairly traded tea, coffee, fruit-juices, and hot chocolate. One had a large cupboard in their coffee bar that opened to create an attractive mini-shop display. Another began a Harambee-type market stall. Another became so committed to Fairtrade that they turned a dry, secure room over to its team who used it and became the distributor of fairly traded goods to new or fledgling stalls in schools, offices, and other churches. But all of these congregations shifted their catering policies to cut out processed foodstuffs, cook from fresh, bottled, canned, or frozen, using as many Fairtrade products as possible—that shared example was replicated in many folks' own households.

Churches can begin to eat together with increasing frequency, both at "cell" and congregational levels.[8] If this is tied in with demonstrably good "whole earth" meals, cooked in the right quantities,[9] with any surpluses sent home with families, lessons about justice and sharing are given without words.

What churches can do is encourage a "theology of enough,"[10] abandoning the false and wrongful teachings of the "prosperity gospel." The biblical call for moderation in an increasingly consumer-oriented society began in the late 1960s. Yet it was not heeded by many pastors, preachers, and denominations and therefore received scant attention except among groups, like Mennonites and Quakers, who had always perceived simple lifestyle as a matter of discipleship. Now, although late in the day, is the time to begin rebuilding a theology of "enough."

Churches in every continent need to recognize their power for change. If our Christian faith understands conversion as *metanoia*, which means "turning around,"[11] we are committed to bringing about change. Probably, one of the biggest theological problems the church faces is to realize that corporate sin subjugating the poor, the alienated, and the starving is just as serious as any individual or personal sin. Institutional and global change is just as vitally part of the church's mission as "saving souls."

8. Francis, *Hospitality and Community*.

9. Good and Stoltzfus, *Mennonite Fellowship Meals*.

10. Taylor, *Enough is Enough*.

11. Krailsheimer, *Conversion*.

That power for change can happen at a variety of levels. Clearly a pastor or priest can lead their congregation into prayerful and biblical reflection, with consequent active discipleship to enable lifestyle and social justice changes. But if vibrant discipleship has already been nurtured, the actions of a small activist "cell" can change the lifestyle of a whole congregation towards socially just "whole earth" patterns of living. Sometimes this will involve enabling many in that congregation to lobby their elected representatives in government, local and national, to work for such social justice.

Partnerships

Do not be frightened of creating alliances with others. Just as the UK Fairtrade Foundation had two of its organizational founders in the more Protestant Christian Aid or the Roman Catholic agency CAFOD, it worked with the non-faith-based charity Oxfam, and the secular National Federation of Women's Institutes. So at a local level we deny ourselves something of God's richness if we will work only with other like-minded Christians.

Deliberately, the small neighborhood group to which I belong includes activist supporters of Amnesty International, Greenpeace, Oxfam, Pax Christi, and Sea Shepherds. Not all are Christians or even theists. Those of us who are disciples of Jesus consciously do not want to work just with "our kind" of Christians. Powerfully, each of these other groups often meet over meals and find themselves asking, "What in God's name *have we* been eating?" even if the majority of others do not believe in God.

We live in a heterogeneous world. Christians, orthodox and radical, believing in a God-in-community, the Trinity, which can be expressed as Creator-Savior-Sustainer. The gospel is for the world of black and white, female and male, slave and free, young and old, that all may discover the God revealed in Jesus who brings "life in all its fullness." A community that is diverse has more chance of exploring common experiences thoroughly enough to build stronger conclusions and outworkings. Dialogue with others is more likely to bring forward change than an arrogant monologue.

Change Your Lifestyle

Wendell Berry, a Kentuckian farmer-philosopher, wrote, "You can eat food by yourself. A meal, according to my understanding anyhow, is a communal event, bringing together family members, neighbors, even strangers."[12] We need to change our lives sufficiently that eating meals together is a frequent occurrence, enabling people to relate together and talk about what really matters.

That is exactly what Wendell and Tanya Berry began to enable when, in 1964, they left behind East Coast academia for a small rundown Midwest farm, where he would have time to write and they would have time to grow "as much of their own food as possible" and to enjoy the company of others. We can all choose to create a life-plan, to downsize even within our own city, to exchange the large mortgage for a "whole earth" lifestyle in mid-town or the suburbs. How many spare cars do you need in your garage? We need to learn how to live "more with less," taking heart that others have done it.[13]

Men need to (re-)learn that their cooking is not confined to the grill/barbecue, but they can and should sous-chef for others, whether preparing raw vegetables or kneading bread. It is OK for an alpha-male to cook for his family or spend a day berry-picking, helping with the gluts or making jams and pickles.

Bake. Even in the most urban, downtown apartment, we can bake bread.[14] The smell of newly baked bread permeates into the hallway or out of the open window, inviting others to inhale, then talk. I have equally rich memories of sharing newly baked bread on the steps of a Bronx housing project, in an English cathedral refectory, with a Greek shepherd at his hillside home, and in many other places. Bread is a great social leveler. John Howard Yoder, the renowned Mennonite theologian, often said, "Bread eaten together is economic sharing . . . that basic needs are met is a sign of the messianic age."[15] The task of Christian people is to declare that messianic age in their daily living.

As we learn to share our bread, we become more than companions on our lives' journey. Would you deny your bread to a starving child? You can change your lifestyle to make a difference.

12. Berry, *Bringing it to the Table*, 185.

13. Longacre, *Living More with Less*.

14. David, *English Bread and Yeast Cookery*.

15. Yoder, *Body Politics*, 20–21.

"Think Global—Act Local"

Nils-Arvid Bringéus, the Swedish ethologist, wrote, "The dining table is the place where material, social and spiritual forces amalgamate"[16]; it will be the place where many of us can most easily discuss two matters with others. The first is our increasing lack of control over our diets if we do not change our priorities in buying or growing what we eat. The second is that during the hour in which that meal has been shared, nine hundred more people will have died of starvation. Hopefully, this book will have enabled you to make more connections between those two facts. These things matter not just because they are issues, but because they affect both this planet and our relationships with other human beings upon it. "Think global—act local."

I listened to a Chicago preacher who told how his congregation abandoned Christmas presents, except for the kids, within families to send the money saved to victims of the New Orleans flood. It was so well-received by his congregation that they now repeat the exercise every other year for international famine relief. Another extended Virginia family send the equivalent of their Thanksgiving dinner costs to an African agricultural charity. We need to make the connections, change our mindsets, and create a fresh heart of committed generosity for God's world and its people.

Can you imagine the change if in each year of your adult life you managed to encourage and persuade just one more person to begin that "Think global—act local" commitment in the way that they eat or respond to this book's global issues and then they began doing the same?

Friends on the Journey

Continually, this chapter has referred to the support and influence of other people as you reshape your life's answer to "What in God's name are we eating?"

Very few of us are called to be hermits. Even fewer are fortunate enough to be on that mythical desert island where crops spring from the ground, fish jump from the sea, and fruit falls from the trees, allowing the hermit to lie in the sun, pray, and contemplate his or her navel. All the rest of us live in an interdependent world, which affects our diet, our living, and our shopping. We all need to foster friendship—even anonymously with our food producers, and with the starving by acting responsibly.

16. Bringéus, *Man, Food and Milieu*, 34.

Although they are both dead now, I used to know two widowed women neighbors in Birmingham, England. One was a white, English, university-educated schoolteacher, the other a Pakistani, village-schooled Muslim; their respective husbands' deaths brought them together as friends. They decided to make a difference and in three separate ways, always together, they invited other women into their homes and started new projects. One was a supporters group for an international charity, another was to help fund a still-ongoing women's refuge, and the third was to visit Pakistan for a few months every other year and work in a women's education project. Their global strategy began as bereaved neighbors.

Developing a global strategy does not need grandiose plans—just a passion and commitment to change things. It also requires us to never forget that when we ask, "What in God's name are we eating?" we have the freedom and good fortune to do so, while one in seven of the rest lives on less than one US dollar a day. Why are you still prevaricating about doing something?

14

Conclusions

WHETHER YOU PICKED UP this book because you wanted just to learn some more about your own daily eating *or* you were already realizing that your consumption had effects on others, we have journeyed to common ground. Even if we eat alone daily or in a noisy household, what we consume has impact upon other individuals and the eco-system of our one and only planet. We never eat in isolation.

Therefore, I offer *seven* simple conclusions about how we respond to that planetary and human interdependence. Each of them challenges our (hopefully past) isolationist consumerism. Each of them contains major implications for our lifestyle and our priorities. Each of them offers a conclusion from a different standpoint:

As individuals, we have to (re-)discover:

- A desire not to return to the quasi-independent, non-cooperative past life.
- A practical commitment to "work" whatever amount of land we are entrusted with.
- A need to rediscover an inner simplicity to "tread lightly upon the land" as thinking global citizens.
- How to use less of the world's resources.
- A commitment to ongoing change.

As consumers, we have to choose and make time to buy the earth-friendly alternatives. We need to shop more carefully and more locally using small specialist traders' and producers' markets. We need to choose the organic and animal-friendly products, eating less but better meat. We need to bake more of our bread and cook as often as possible from good, raw ingredients, rejecting the processed and "ready meal" alternatives. Buy as many fairly traded items as you will use fully. Put on extra clothes rather than use more fuel. Clean and wash with earth-friendly products. Adopt a "whole earth" lifestyle.

As households, we need to advance that "whole earth" lifestyle. This means not needing the latest kitchen gadgets or even the latest kitchen or car or to fly across the world too often. It means being generous, giving away our spare furniture and unused clothes, risking lending our books, CDs, DVDs, and tools, and even considering how we can share the extra space in our homes. Why not create a local "collective" who can share expensive tools, food gluts, labor, and a variety of vehicles? Ensure that your backyard can produce food. Live the alternative lifestyle together.

Churches at every level—"cell," congregationally, denominationally, and internationally—need to ignite and foster a debate, within and beyond the Christian spectrum, as well as theological study and discipleship's activism, about the nature of *oikos*. This Greek word, meaning household, gives the root of English-language words such as economy, ecology, and ecumenical—concepts that have global significance in their interaction. The prophetic voice and life of every Christian, both individually and within their faith communities, needs to challenge populations, politicians, and governments to recognize that set of *oikos* interrelationships and to respond to the benefit of all global citizens.

As democratic voters, we have to be prepared to mobilize, to lobby our elected representatives again, then again. We must be prepared to let go of some of our party allegiances in order to ensure that at every level of our own country's government there are "thinking voices" committed to global change. If they are really committed to a "whole earth" lifestyle for all, they will not be worried about personal wealth or becoming a career politician. From the global stage, think Mahatma Gandhi, Aung San Suu Kyi, think Ed de la Torre, Desmond Tutu, think Angela Merkel, Caroline Lucas . . . and your choice is?

As world citizens, we need continually to re-educate ourselves about climate change, eco-concerns, the needs of the developing world and its population, so that we can affect change, reducing our planetary footprint. It begins with reviewing how we live and eat—the central seven "big issue" chapters of this book can kick-start that personal and collective discussion. It means never being content with the status quo . . . it means nurturing more selfless friendships and behavior while challenging the selfish and greedy. It means that other people matter just as much as we do. The wisest universal teacher once said, "Love your neighbor as yourself."

As those made in the "image of God," we cannot afford to ignore all of the above. We are stewards and now co-creators of the world that is coming. God began with a garden full of provision and brings it to fruition in a bedazzling city where all have place in a vision of peace and plenty. Humankind began in a planet full of provision. Whether we bring it to its conclusion in a warring dustbowl, with the starving and the subjugated scattered to the margins, or whether we turn around (*metanoia* again) and re-establish that vision and society of peace and plenty, the choice is in our own hearts, minds, and hands.

The choice is yours.

Just one step starts a journey. Just one helping hand can pull someone from the mire. Just one new friendship can be an example to so many others. Just one . . . and will that one be yours?

Bibliography

Internet searches can easily bring up the factual information one might wish to have regarding agriculture, animal welfare, ecology, population figures, and trade issues. The following are predominantly books that provide thinking to enable you to continue your reflection and activism, having read this book.

Bakke, Ray. *The Urban Christian*. Leicester, UK: InterVarsity, 1987.

Berry, Wendell. *The Art of the Commonplace*. Emeryville, CA: Shoemaker & Hoard, 2002.

———. *Bringing It to the Table*. Berkeley, CA: Counterpoint, 2009.

———. "The Pleasures of Eating." In *Simpler Living, Compassionate Life: A Christian Perspective*, edited by M. Schut, 105–10. Denver: Moorhouse Group, 1999.

Brandt, Willy. *North-South: A Program for Survival*. Boston: MIT, 1990.

Bringéus, Nils-Arvid. *Man, Food and Milieu*. Edinburgh: Tuckwell, 2001.

Cairney, Edward. *The Sprouters Handbook*. Glendaruel, UK: Argyll, 1997.

Chanda, Nayan. *Bound Together: How Traders, Preachers, Adventurers and Warriors Shaped Globalization*. New Haven: Yale University Press, 2007.

Chang, Jung, and Jon Halliday. *Mao: The Unknown Story*. Sydney: Random House, 2006.

Colqhoun, Kate. *The Thrifty Cookbook: 476 Ways to Eat Well with Leftovers*. London: Bloomsbury, 2010.

Corbin, Pam. *Preserves*. New York: Bloomsbury/River Cottage, 2008.

Crossan, John Dominic. *The Historical Jesus: The Life of a Mediterranean Jewish Peasant*. San Francisco: Harper, 1992.

Daly, Herman E., and John B. Cobb. *For the Common Good: Re-directing the Economy toward Community, Environment and a Sustainable Future*. Boston: Beacon, 1989.

David, Elizabeth. *English Bread and Yeast Cookery*. London: Penguin, 1979.

De Botton, Alain. *Religion for Atheists: A Non-believer's Guide to the Uses of Religion*. London: Hamish Hamilton, 2012.

Deane-Drummond, Celia. *Eco-Theology*. London: Darton, Longman, & Todd, 2008.

Despommier, Dickson. *The Vertical Farm: Feeding the World in the Twenty-First Century*. New York: Dunne, 2010.

Diacono, Mark. *Veg Patch.* New York: Bloomsbury/River Cottage, 2008.

Dunn, Marilyn. *The Emergence of Monasticism from the Desert Fathers until the Early Middle Ages.* Oxford: Blackwell, 2003.

Ehrlich, Paul. *The Population Bomb.* London: Macmillan, 1971.

Elliott, Charles. *Comfortable Compassion.* Sydney: Hodder, 1987.

Elliot, Rose. *The Bean Book.* Glasgow: Fontana, 1979.

Erasmus, Udo. *Fats that Heal, Fats that Kill.* Burnaby, BC: Alive, 1993.

Fisher-McGarry, Julie. *Be the Change You Want to See in the World.* Berkeley, CA: Conari, 2006.

Flowerdew, Bob. *Bob Flowerdew's Organic Bible.* London: Kyle Cathie, 1998.

———. *Composting.* London: Kyle Cathie, 2010.

Francis, Andrew. *Hospitality and Community After Christendom.* Milton Keynes, UK: Paternoster, 2012.

———. "How Then Shall We Eat?" PhD diss., Princeton University, 2010.

———. *The Wind of the Spirit: How British Church History Shaped Faith and Spirituality.* Leeds, UK: HHSC, 2000.

George, Susan. *Feeding the Few: Corporate Control of Food.* London: Penguin, 1985.

———. *How the Other Half Dies: The Real Reasons for World Hunger.* London: Penguin, 1980.

Ghazi, Polly, and Judy Jones. *Downshifting.* London: Coronet, 1997.

Good, Phyllis Pellman, and Louise Stoltzfus. *The Best of Mennonite Fellowship Meals.* Intercourse, PA: Good Books, 1991.

Grigson, Sophie, and William Black. *Fish.* London: Headline, 1998.

Jaffray, Madhur. *Indian Cookery.* Sydney: Random House, 1990.

Kiple, Kenneth F. *A Moveable Feast: Ten Millennia of Food Globalisation.* Cambridge: Cambridge University Press, 2007.

Krailsheimer, A. J. *Conversion.* London: SCM, 1980.

Lawrence, Felicity. *Eat Your Heart Out.* New York: Penguin, 2008.

———. *Not On the Label.* London: Penguin, 2004.

Longacre, Doris Janzen. *Living More with Less.* Scottdale, PA: Herald, 1995.

———. *More-with-Less Cookbook.* Scottdale, PA: Herald, 1990.

Mabey, Richard. *Food for Free.* London: Collins, 2007.

Malthus, Thomas. *An Essay on the Principle of Population.* Edited by Geoffrey Gilbert. Oxford: Oxford University Press, 2008.

McFague, Sallie. *Life Abundant.* Minneapolis: Fortress, 2000.

———. *Models of God: Theology for an Ecological, Nuclear Age.* Minneapolis: Fortress, 1987.

McGinnis, James B. *Bread and Justice: Toward a New International Economic Order.* New York: Paulist, 1979.

McLuhan, Marshall. *The Global Village.* New York: Oxford University Press, 2001.

Meadows, Peter. *Rich Thinking about the World's Poor.* Waynesboro, GA: Authentic Lifestyle, 2003.

Mehta, Ved. *Mahatma Gandhi and His Apostles.* London: Penguin, 1976.

Mollison, Bill. *Introduction to Permaculture.* Tyalgum, NSW: Tagari, 1991.

———. *Permaculture: A Designer's Manual.* Tyalgum, NSW: Tagari, 1988.

Morgan, Dan. *Merchants of Grain.* New York: Viking, 1979.

Moules, Noel. *Fingerprints of Fire, Footprints of Peace.* Washington, DC: Circle, 2012.

Murray, Stuart, and Sian Murray Williams. *Multi-Voiced Church.* Milton Keynes, UK: Paternoster, 2012.

Newman, Lucile F. *Hunger in History: Food Shortage, Poverty and Deprivation.* Oxford: Blackwell, 1990.

Nyerges, Christopher, and Dolores Lynn Nyerges. *Extreme Simplicity: Homesteading in the City.* White River Junction, VT: Chelsea Green, 2002.

Obama, Barack. *The Audacity of Hope.* New York: Three Rivers, 2006.

Pasternak, Boris. *Dr. Zhivago.* London: Sphere, 1970.

Pohl, Christine D. *Making Room: Recovering Hospitality as a Christian Tradition.* Grand Rapids: Eerdmans, 1999.

Rieger, Joerg. *Liberating the Future.* Minneapolis: Fortress, 1998.

Rotberg, Robert L., and Theodore K. Rabb. *Hunger and History: The Impact of Changing Food Production and Consumption Patterns on Society.* Cambridge: Cambridge University Press, 1995.

Rubinstein, Helge, and Sheila Bush. *The Penguin Freezer Cookbook.* Harmondsworth, UK: Penguin, 1973.

Scheier, Joan. *New York City Zoos and Aquarium.* Charleston, SC: Arcadia, 2005.

Schlabach, Joetta Hendrick. *Extending the Table.* Scottdale, PA: Herald, 1991.

Schumacher, E. F. *Small Is Beautiful.* London: Abacus, 1974.

Scott-Heron, Gil. "The Revolution Will Not Be Televised." In *Now and Then: The Poems of Gil Scott-Heron*, 77–79. Edinburgh: Canongate, 2000.

Seymour, John. *The Complete Book of Self-Sufficiency.* London: Faber, 1976.

Smil, Vaclav. *Enriching the Earth: Fritz Haber, Carl Bosch and the Transformation of World Food Production.* Cambridge: MIT, 2004.

Smith, Delia. *One Is Fun!* London: Hodder & Stoughton, 1985.

Sprott, W. J. H. *Human Groups.* London: Pelican, 1970.

Standage, John. *An Edible History of Humanity.* New York: Walker, 2009.

Steinbeck, John. *Cannery Row.* London: Heinemann, 1963.

———. *The Grapes of Wrath.* London: Heinemann, 1939.

Stevens, Daniel. *Bread.* River Cottage Handbook 3. New York: Bloomsbury/River Cottage, 2009.

Tansey, Geoff, and Tony Worsley. *The Food System.* London: Earthscan, 1995.

Taylor, John V. *Enough Is Enough.* London: SCM, 1975.

Van Olphem, Bart, and Tom Kime. *Fish Tales: Stories and Recipes from Sustainable Fisheries and the World.* London: Kyle Cathie, 2009.

Ward, Barbara, and Rene Dubos. *Only One Earth.* New York: Norton, 1972.

Webb, Stephen H. *Good Eating.* Grand Rapids: Brazos, 2001.

Whitehorn, Katherine. *Cooking in a Bedsitter.* London: Penguin, 1970.

Wright, John. *Edible Seashore.* London: Bloomsbury, 2009.

———. *Hedgerow.* River Cottage Handbook 7. London: Bloomsbury, 2011.

Yoder, John Howard. *Body Politics.* Nashville: Discipleship Resources, 1997.

———. *For the Nations.* Grand Rapids: Eerdmans, 1997.

79500895R00105

Made in the USA
San Bernardino, CA
14 June 2018